# U2

*The Story so Far*

# U2

*The Story so Far*

by

Richard Seal

*BRITANNIA PRESS PUBLISHING*

First published in Great Britain in 1993.

British Library Cataloguing in Publication Data. A Catalogue record for this book is available from the British Library.

Seal.
U2 - *The Story so Far*

ISBN 0-9519937-2-0 (Paperback)

Printed and bound in Great Britain by Biddles Ltd, Surrey.
All photographs: Rex Features Ltd.

Britannia Press Publishing, Britannia Crest International Ltd
27A James Street, The Piazza, Covent Garden, London WC2E 8PA.

# Contents

## About the Author

Richard Seal was born near Sevenoaks, Kent in 1966. For the past eight years, he has worked within the music industry, starting as a CD buyer for Virgin Megastore. He then worked as a consultant for 35mm Music helping to compile original soundtrack albums for films, moving onto work in the A &R Department of Warner Chappell Music for two years. Subsequently left to pursue a career as a freelance journalist and music writer. His latest work was to compile classic QUEEN material for inclusion on the soundtrack of a forthcoming Walt Disney film.

# Introduction

From small time local talent contest winners in their native home of Dublin, Ireland, U2 have gone on to reach a pinnacle of achievement in the Rock music world.

Opening with their encouraging debut album, 'Boy', full of youthful enthusiasm and promise, they have progressed musically with such albums as the more thoughtful and reflective "October", the bold and forthright 'War', the smooth excesses of 'The Unforgettable Fire', the multi million selling, ultimate world wide breakthrough of 'The Joshua Tree', the searching and acknowledging 'Rattle And Hum', up to the present day with perhaps their most critically acclaimed and experimental album to date, 'Achtung Baby', which saw them flirt with a new dance element to their music, and emerge triumphant.

From small clubs to occasionally unremarkable sized audience, they now find themselves in the position, that in order to justify the demand to see them, they are scheduled to play live to a potential audience of over 260,000 fans, over a four nights period, in London this summer. A far cry from the nine that attended that concert at London's The Hope And Anchor some fourteen years ago.

They have not been afraid to experiment or change their musical output and style over the years as, *'Achtung Baby'* so readily illustrates. And with that album and the subsequent 'Zoo TV' live concert dates to accompany it, they have reached a whole new peak of achievement, as well as critical and commercial success. This includes their being named as the top grossing live Rock band of the year in America for 1992, allegedly taking an incredible $63.8 million dollars from seventy concerts there that year.

They have never been afraid to speak their minds, and show a great knowledge and understanding about a variety of such diverse subjects as pollution and potential nuclear contamination, wrongful political imprisonment and the situations that prevail on their own doorsteps in their native Ireland. People might not always agree with what they have said, but they've always sat up, taken note and listened.

U2 write songs that are meaningful and thought provoking; many of their songs over the years have quite rightly been regarded as classic moments, for many different reasons, and to many different people. Often able to capture a mood, a moment or a feeling and portray it so well.

Their careers have had many highs. A triumphant performance at Live Aid, ground breaking success in America at the concerts to celebrate Amnesty International's Twenty-fifth anniversary, as well as headlining many huge sell out concerts in their own right.

A variety of prestigious awards have been bestowed on the group. At the 1993 Brit Awards they were presented with the award for Best Live act in the world today, and at the Grammy's, *'Achtung Baby'* was honoured for Best Rock Vocal Performance.

*'The Story So Far'* is just that, from those early meanderings when they were just another band, whom no one particularly predicted great things and much of a future for, to the present day, when whatever your opinion of them, you cannot escape or ignore them and their influence.

# Chapter 1

## Full Of Youthful Exuberance

Contrary to the widely held popular belief of many neutral observers, not all the members of U2 were actually born in Ireland. Dave Evans was born at Barking Maternity Hospital in Essex, England on the 8th August, 1961, while Adam Clayton was born in Chinnor in Oxfordshire, England on March 13th, 1960.

Dave Evans parents Garvin and Gwenda were, very much as their names suggest, of Welsh descent. A year after his birth, the family moved to Malahide, a middle class coastal town about eight miles from the centre of Dublin with a large Protestant community. He had a pleasant, conventional childhood and upbringing along with his brother Dick and sister Gill. His father was an active participant, singing in various Welsh male voice choirs, and his mother was a competent piano player, so music in one form or another surrounded Dave from an early age.

Adam Clayton's father Brian was a Royal Air Force pilot. After accepting a position at Aer Lingus, based in Ireland, the family up-rooted and moved to Dublin when Adam was five years of age. Like the Evans' they also settled in Malahide where Adam spent a rather solitary childhood, preferring his own company, wandering around the largely isolated beaches, visiting his grand-parents who had also moved there, or investigating the woodlands around the town's imposing castle. He ended up at Mount Temple school after a largely unhappy spell at Castle Park in Dalkey, near Dublin Bay (a relatively local boarding school) which upheld traditional teaching and discipline values. He then went on to St. Columba's College, Rathfarham, which is where he first developed an interest in music; this was the only true benefit of his time there, as he did not particularly shine academically or on a disciplinarian level.

Paul Hewson was born on 10th May, 1960 at Rotunda hospital in Dublin, to parents Iris and Bobby. He has one brother, Norman who is seven years older than himself.

Despite his parents' mixed marriage (his father was Catholic, his mother Church of Ireland Protestant), it had been decided to raise Paul the same way as they had his brother, in the Protestant faith. In his early years, this often led to inner conflict, as he felt somehow detached, a catholic, masquerading as a Protestant.

He pursued all the normal childhood activities but was conspicuously more interested in artistic, rather than the more readily accepted sporty pursuits. He was a popular child mixing with other children of the neighbourhood, forming friendships and allegiances, whatever their particular religious beliefs may have been.

After primary school when the time came to enter higher education, he had wanted to attend the same high school as his brother had done. But Norman had won a scholarship, and without such aid the fees for this were beyond the resources of Bobby and Iris Hewsons. After a time of discussion and conflict over which school of higher education he would attend, the subject of Mount Temple came up, which is really where the story begins.

Mount Temple was something of an exception within the strict and domineering Irish Education system, providing a rare and fortuitously liberal way of teaching and learning, this proved ideal for the development of interests and pursuits outside of the usual school curriculum. Such formalities as uniforms were dispensed with, the regime was not merely that you were there to be taught but were actively encouraged to participate your own ideas and thoughts; an ideal breeding ground for originality. Mount Temple was also to be the learning platform for the education of Larry Mullen.

Larry Mullen was born 1st October, 1961. An average student academically, he was however set aside from others by his classic good looks and shoulder length blond hair. He was born and raised around Dublin and lived during his attendance there just a mile from Mount Temple school in Artane.

He became interested in music and particularly the drums at an early age. He took lessons to develop his technique and would closely scrutinise performances of other drummers. This would usually take the form of playing along to the appearances of the glam rock greats of the time such as The Sweet and Slade's regular performances on Top Of The Pops. However, musically speaking he learnt far more from pursuing his own improvisations where his drumming was concerned.

After a couple of enjoyable and beneficial stints with outfits such as The Post Office Workers Union Band, he had gathered enough confidence in himself and his playing to take things a step further, and to go about the business of setting up his own band.

Once the idea of setting up his own band had taken a hold on the young Larry Mullen, he set about the task of enlisting his recruits for this venture. He had been greatly inspired to do this by the enormous success many bands from Ireland, such as, Thin Lizzy, The Undertones and The BoomTown Rats were having overseas and at home during this time. This provided the necessary inspiration for him to seriously consider doing it for himself. Although he initially got almost no response from this note he eventually assembled together five hopefuls who all wanted to play lead guitar.

Their first impromptu performance together was in Larry's kitchen where they stumbled their way through a couple of unorthodox sounding versions of The Rolling Stones' classics, 'Satisfaction' and Brown Sugar'. The coveted role of playing lead guitar was eventually bestowed upon Dave Evans after he gave an impressive rendition of the Taste song 'Blister on the Moon'. Larry's role as drummer was already confirmed, and it became clear that Paul Hewson was far better at communicating through his mouth than with the aid of an instrument, which would of course eventually lead to him taking up the mantle of lead vocalist. Adam, of course, was eventually to master the art of playing bass guitar.

The band initially named themselves Feedback, due to what more often than not was emitted from Adam's guitar amp. This name did not last long and they were soon to be renamed 'The Hype', this in turn, was eventually to be overshadowed by the idea suggested by band friend Steve Averill, (then singer with the intriguingly named 'Radiators From Space'), that they should be christened with the very simple but effectively sounding name of U2. It stuck and the story started to evolve. With the help of one of their teachers at Mount Temple they were able to get the use of a spare room at the school where they could rehearse.

As in many teenage situations, bonds are formed, allegiances made and gangs or societies are created. One such existed at Mount Temple school at the time.

'The Village' or 'Lipton Village' as it was also known, was a refuge for a set of like minded individuals to distance themselves somewhat from the tiresome conventions and every day routine of Dublin life. It became their own name for Dublin. The main core of 'The Village' consisted of members from U2 themselves and some other Dublin teenagers, one of whom was Gavin Friday, (who went on to achieve cult success as lead singer of The Virgin Prunes, and as a solo artist). Members of 'The Village' were set aside from their contemporaries and would engage in mutual activities apart from the norm.

Being a member of 'The Village', and consequently having to be rechristened with a pseudonym as part of the criteria for entry, is how Paul Hewson was eventually set to become Bonovox, or Bono for short. This was inspired by a sign seen on what turned out to be a hearing aid shop in O'Connell street in Dublin. Although he was not officially looked upon as being a member of this elite group, Dave Evans was also bestowed with the honour of receiving a pseudonym. This was created by Bono who rechristened him 'Edge', due to his being in possession of a sharp mind and wily instincts.

Despite their very varied musical influences and having various areas of incompetence in their chosen musical roles, Larry, Adam Bono and The Edge found they shared enough mutual determination to pursue vigorously this new found interest in music.

Their first live public performance together was at Mount Temple school in 1978. It was a big success, and Bono was later heard to comment that it would be another two years before they would match that initial performance together which he described as *"one of the greatest gigs we ever played"*.

With this new found optimism and confidence came the inevitable succession of playing together live, when and where they could. This helped them to create a reputation for themselves as being a good night's entertainment, and an alternative to the usual Dublin teenage pursuit of hanging around the local pubs.

The gigs were forthcoming, never particularly difficult to obtain, but often taking place in the most unconventional of surroundings, such as, on one occasion, when they were booked to play in the somewhat unglamorous setting of a local car-park.

As their reputation began to grow and the gigs became better and better attended, they started to realise the potential of what they were doing. Bono commented some years later on the situation, saying, *"we were a shambles compared to the professional and heavy rock bands, but I knew we had something. I knew the effect we had over the audience. Even though we were technically lacking, we had a spark: we built around that spark."*

That "spark" was confirmed when they won a talent contest held by Guinness and Harp, which they had only entered in the first place as a bit of a joke. This, though, would help them to eventually land a small recording contract with the Irish Division of CBS Records.

Although there were many great moments during these formative years there were also a few disasters.

Like many of their contemporaries they started out in the early days by playing a variety of cover versions, but they soon realised that they were pretty hopeless at playing other people's songs, so were forced to set about the task of writing some of their own. With their influences being so varied this often resulted in a very ramshackle sound emerging. Whilst admiring songwriters in the John Lennon mould, they found they couldn't collectively particularly identify with the somewhat hippy attitudes that more often than not accompanied it.

Punk, which had exploded onto the music scene in 1976 again appealed to them in the way that it had many others, being impressed with its rawness and sense of abandon. But the trimmings involved, the anarchic lifestyle, being cut free of any moral or religious conventions did not appeal.

Their musical growth has often been phenomenal, occasionally stagnant, but rarely dull. Very much in the mould of a traditional rock band, their arrival onto this scene came at very much the right time. Although subsequently over the years they have incorporated many and varied influences, everyone from Elvis and Bob Dylan up to Blues and Gospel, their enduring and particularly their early appeal lay very much in good, strong, competent live performances.

Without surrounding themselves with gimmicks or other such

props they were able to communicate with the audience through the songs, dealing with issues on a personal level that others could relate to, and on a more general level, with events within the world that the audience could identify and perhaps sympathise with.

With this growing reputation came the need to develop in other areas, and on board came Paul McGuiness to undertake managerial duties.

He had been reluctant to even go and see them at first, but actually expressed an interest in managing them from the first night he saw them playing live in a small Dublin club called The Project in May, 1978.

He set about the task of setting them up with a record deal, which in a clever move was only to be for Ireland. Nothing would yet be released in the UK or elsewhere.

This first release was a three track EP named U23 on the CBS/Ireland label in September 1979.

A clever marketing trick was employed for the release with only 1,000 copies being made available. This was not only to guarantee publicity for the release but would inevitably create a soon to be collectors' item at the same time.

The main track chosen to front this EP was 'Out Of Control'. It was written on Bono's 18th birthday and the lyrics of the song was concerned with what Bono had stated were the two most important things in one's life which ultimately you had no control over, life and death.

This track was chosen over 'Stories For Boys' which was preferred by some as it had a more instant quality about it, with a much more pop-orientated sound.

Produced by Chas de Whalley, this limited and numbered release gained a favourable review in Ireland's leading rock magazine 'The Hot Press',(who were to be an important ally to U2 in the early days), and eventually was to go on and become a fair sized hit in Ireland.

Although the single was generally well received, the group themselves were not particularly impressed with the finished product, which later would be rerecorded for their debut album. Bono said of the original version of the song at the time, *"I remember when I first heard it, I just wanted to stand on the bridge in O'Connell Street, and jump into the river,"* such was his disappointment with the finished result.

Not everyone, however, was so distraught, particularly not the fans, as in January of 1980 U2 were to win five categories in The Hot Press readers' poll.

Around this time they made their first tentative steps at playing outside of Ireland. This included a gig at The Rock Garden in London's Covent Garden, and also a surely memorable if somewhat under attended appearance at The Hope and Anchor, also in London, where only nine paying customers turned up to watch the group in action. A far more disappointing aspect about this in real terms, however, was that they received little if any music press coverage about the gigs, and so, still, very few people knew who they were outside their native Ireland.

Part of the reason for these London gigs was to try and set up a deal for the group outside of Ireland. However, the general indifference shown to the group by the British audiences, and disasters such as at 'The Hope and Anchor', didn't exactly help the situation. They were destined to return to Ireland without the hoped for record deal they sought emerging. They had also made the conscious decision as a group, despite a lot of intervention from neutral observers, to stay in Ireland and not up root themselves and be based in London, which was so often the expected norm, and as many had suggested.

With the return to Dublin came a proposed Irish tour. They decided that with the lack of interest generated elsewhere they should concentrate for the time being on Ireland where in the eyes of the Irish public they were a big attraction.

To accompany this tour they recorded their second single *'Another Day'* which was released in February of 1980. It was criticised in reviews as being poorly produced and attaining a somewhat juvenile sound, completely failing to capture or capitalise on the group's by now euphoric live performances. The single was again released only in Ireland on CBS Records small division there.

The need to sign a record deal outside of Ireland was now the all consuming preoccupation within the U2 camp. The need to venture abroad and to conquer other markets became of utmost importance. They had captured and created a dedicated and loyal following in Ireland, but still meant little elsewhere. This was eventually achieved after a triumphant homecoming gig at the 2,000 capacity National Boxing Stadium on Dublin's South Circular road.

After the gig, they were offered a deal on the spot by Bill Stewart of Island Records, one of the few major labels at the time to realise their enormous potential at an early stage. They were offered a four year, four album deal and just as importantly, the promise of financial support for tours of territories outside of the United Kingdom.

Their first release for the then Chris Blackwell owned Island Record label was "*11 O'Clock, Tick, Tock*'.

The song was produced by Martin Hannett ( now sadly deceased), famed for his early work with The Teardrop Explodes and production of the Joy Division album '*Unknown Pleasures*'.

'*11 O'Clock, Tick, Tock*' proved to be far more satisfying than previously released material. They were able to utilise the potential of the studio far more than before, and this certainly showed on the end result. It proved to be a somewhat one off release for U2, particularly sound wise, much darker than previous material and certainly different from what was eventually to follow.

The group then spent most of the summer of 1980 touring around Britain, playing small sized venues and building up a following.

The next single release was '*A Day Without Me*' in August, 1980. It didn't fare particularly well in the charts, although releasing a song with suicide as the lyrical theme obviously doesn't guarantee a lot of peak time radio play. The main plus point of the single's release from the groups point of view though, was that it was their first real studio recording that went some way to capturing how they sounded live, which at the time was very much their biggest selling point.

'*A Day Without Me*' was their first recording with Steve Lillywhite as producer, who would subsequently go on to produce their first three albums.

# Chapter 2

## A Finger in The Pie

October of 1980 was to herald the release of U2's debut album 'Boy'.

The album's front cover soon became one of the most talked about of the year. Containing no words, it showed just a photography of the head and shoulders of an innocent looking young boy. This was to generate interest in many ways that had certainly not been intended. There was a lot of talk,(particularly in America where the cover was changed), of the picture having paedophile or gay connotations, where in reality its purpose was merely to represent the album's main themes of childhood, innocence, sensuality and temptation.

The album was hugely acclaimed by critics and the public alike, the songs, a combination of new material and live favourites, were strong, direct and vibrant.

The album opened with the instantaneous guitar hook and crashing drum sound of '*I Will Follow*'. Although the song was merely a mixture of simple hooks and melodies, immediately the band's potential was becoming evident. Their originality was certainly not in question. The sound that the band had created was quite unlike anything else around at the time. The biggest and most successful bands of this period were undoubtedly The Police, The Jam and Blondie, but the group had made no conscious decision to sound like any of these; instead there was an 'underground' feel to the music which had far more in common with other cult groups of the time such as Echo And The Bunnymen and Joy Division.

Indeed '*Twilight*', the album's second track, was not dissimilar sound wise to the music that Echo And The Bunnymen were making at the time.

The next track '*An Cat Dubh*' had a bass guitar hook that was not a million miles away from being a slowed down version of The Knack's '*My Sharona*', although that song itself had blatantly borrowed sounds from many of its predecessors.

Slight nods were made towards punk with the album's rerecorded versions of '*Out Of Control*' and '*Stories For Boys*'.

'*Out Of Control*' still sounding fresh and exciting, part of its appeal being that the group were not able to fully utilise the potential of the studio, so giving the track its rawness. The same went for '*Stories For Boys*' with its lyrical tales of schoolboy fantasies and escaping to imaginary places. Whilst this slight appreciation of punk was indicated by the sound of both '*Out Of Control*' and '*Stories For Boys*', both of them had a slightly better sense of melody than many of the punk reactionaries were able to conjure up on their records.

'*The Ocean*' was no more than a short interlude which was pleasant enough, without being particularly earth-shattering, suffering somewhat by the vocals being too far back in the mix.

Another breath of fresh air followed however with the single '*A Day Without Me*', still retaining its sense of abandon and childhood naivete, which had originally so adequately set it apart from other records.

'*Another Time, Another Place*', if given the beefier sounding production that it yearned for, would not have seemed out of place if played in the huge football stadiums the band would eventually end up playing.

Many of the album's tracks contained, and were undoubtedly influential upon, the clattering drum and jangly guitar sounds that would dominate the huge indie scene that was to flourish in subsequent years.

'*The Electric Co*' was another simple and yet effective riff-driven song, it was impossible not to tap a foot or bang a pencil in mock imitation of the drum sound it contained.

The album's final track, '*Shadows And Tall Trees*' had a slightly stranger, far more experimental feel to it, and although its execution was not completely successful, by now it was near impossible to find any major faults in what had been an exceptional and highly original debut album. Bono's vocals, and to a lesser degree, the bands musical output, did not yet have the power and authority that would come in later years, and yet they were still original and strong enough within themselves to be set aside from many of their contemporaries.

The reviews upon its release were more than encouraging, with many hailing it as one of the best debut albums of the past decade.

The sound that the group and producer Steve Lillywhite had captured on '*Boy*' was on the whole fresh and raw, as their live shows at the time were, and whilst not quite capturing the sense of abandon that was a feature of the live performances the sound was still distinctive and original enough to be quite unlike anything else around at the time. Here was a band just beginning to find their feet with seemingly effortless composure.

After the release of '*Boy*', U2 were set to undertake their first American concerts, a short series of club dates on the east coast in November of 1980.

During this visit to America they went to Island Records Nassau Studio Complex to record '*Fire*', which proved to be their first major foray into the British Singles chart, eventually providing them with their first Top 40 hit.

That first American tour, which preceded the recording of "*Fire*' was in many ways a huge success, sowing the seeds of what was to grow to hugely magnified proportions in subsequent years.

The shows were said to be excellent, the audience soon being taken into U2's world of passion and exuberance, with the group fully enjoying and taking advantage of this new found alliance.

Still only 19, things were starting to happen in a big way for Bono and the others.

They had released a very well received debut album, made a very beneficial trip to the States, and played a large amount of successful gigs. They also played their first major London headlining show at the Lyceum Ballroom in the Strand, where not only was the show a complete sell out but some 700 people were locked out, such was the demand to see them.

Around this time they also made their first British television appearance on the legendary Old Grey Whistle Test, the day after which they flew back to America for a three months tour.

This second US tour which finished in May, again proved to be hugely successful, ending with concerts at the prestigious New York Palladium and at the Santa Monica Civic Centre.

The support they were beginning to gather in America helped the *'Boy'* album to make a small impact on the American Billboard album chart, and they picked up a lot of useful radio support from independent and college radio stations.

# Chapter 3


## Exorcising Ghosts


Following on from this new found success the time had come to begin recording their second album.

Made in the summer and released ironically in October of 1981, 'October' the album, signalled a marked contrast in its lyrical themes from their debut, shifting uneasily between the thoughts and changes brought on by this new found rock 'n' roll lifestyle and the group's musings on their own religious beliefs and yearnings.

Along with these at times overbearing religious themes, bought on in part by the involvement of Bono, the Edge and Larry with a local Christian group called Shalom, the album was in parts harder and more heavily guitar orientated, without necessarily being melodic, than what had come before.

It was criticised at the time for being over ambitious, The

Edge's guitar playing being put too much forward, consequently being overbearing on some of the tracks.

The album did posses its quieter moments though, predominantly on Side 2, which was a far more erratic affair than what had come before.

The album, in its original form, ("BCD", Before Compact Discs), seemed to take conscientiously different paths on its two sides.

The first being a more straight forward approach and more readily identifiable as being made by U2.

However, side 1 of the album had its weaker moments such as the second track in *'I Fall Down'*, a piano dominant song that had ambitions both musically and vocally but did not really succeed in either areas. It came across like an attempt to invoke some form of high drama and tension into the proceedings but actually ended up as rather too much like amateur dramatics.

*'I Threw A Brick'* started quite strangely, its opening drum pattern sounding not unlike something that would be more easily accommodated on Fleetwood Mac's *'Tusk'* album. It was a disappointingly insubstantial sounding record though. It seemed as though at times the group had inventive and strong enough sounding ideas for their music, but were ultimately unable to decide how far to take and in what way to develop them. *'I Threw A Brick'* was a prime example of this, the potential was so obviously there but expanding and utilising this potential proved to be more of a problem.

*'Rejoice'*, though, is as cliche ridden as the title would suggest, a far more uplifting and satisfying affair. A veritable feast of pounding drums, jangly guitar work and soaring vocals made it, apart from perhaps the singles, by far one of the album's more easily accessible and enjoyable tracks. It had a more readily constructed quality, and despite the heavy use of The Edge's guitar sound, a more melodic one.

Also on Side 1 of the album was *'Fire'*, the song the group had recorded whilst at the Compass Point Studios in Nassau in the Bahamas.

*'Fire'* was one of the albums undoubted highlights. The single had initially paved the way for the album's imminent release and whilst not hinting at any great radical departures for the group, its presence did seem to suggest that they were becoming more knowledgeable and comfortable within their studio based work. The single had a much crisper and sharper sound than anything else on the album and despite its occasional loose feel was actually

a much tighter sounding single than any of its predecessors.

Although it did not exactly set the charts alight it did make in-roads into the Top 40 of the British Single charts and helped to pave the way for what was to come.

*'Fire'* was the track on the album which most accurately rep-resented in many ways what was to later develop, in a musical sense, on future recordings, particularly on the *'War'* album.

Side 2 of *'October'*, however, is a far more patchy affair and is a little disappointing, (save for two tracks), having no real defini-tion or direction meandering along the songs, on the whole weak and disappointing.

One of the notable exceptions though is the first track, *'To-morrow'*. The song starts off very slowly and quietly with just the sound of Bono's voice and some Uillean pipes, before building into a powerful and emotive paean, the lyrics reflecting the turmoil and upset that Bono had felt when confronted by the reality of his mother's death on the day of her funeral. His reluctance to believe that his mother had really died was dealt and fought with in the lyrical twists and questions they posed. The song was dedicated to both his mother (Iris Hewson), and Jesus Christ, who is directly addressed in the last line of the song; it was by far and away one of the most moving songs on the album and indeed one of the more easily accessible tracks on side 2.

*'With A Shout, (Jerusalem)'* starts off very promisingly with its rushing drum beat and familiar guitar led sound, but this in turn actually leads to its down fall. Its main fault is that it is too obviously a U2 record, very nearly bordering in fact on a sort of U2-by-numbers approach. It offers much but unfortunately doesn't ultimately go anywhere. It comes across as being far too definitely structured, throwing in all the little touches and familiarities so readily associated with the 'U2 sound' of around this time.

*'Stranger In A Strange Land'* suffers from much the same problems as *'With A Shout'*, both pleasing enough but ultimately both of them being inoffensively, indifferent tracks. It also appears to be lacking in direction, despite having some nice atmospheric qualities. The lyrics are interesting enough to provoke thoughts and images in one's mind, but the song's general lack of definition means it just peters out towards the end having not fully established its potential worthiness.

*'Scarlet'* has some nice piano, guitar and drum work but the lyrical contribution, which merely consists of Bono singing the refrain 'Rejoice' over and over again doesn't go anywhere near towards adding enough substance to the song in the end. It all

comes across in the end as being a bit too much like a nicely thought up idea for a song, that is competently structured and delivered, but which has no real justifiable existence; perhaps it would have been better hidden away on a B-side of one of the singles.

The other undoubted highlight on Side 2 of '*October*', however, is most certainly the album's title track. The song is a genuine surprise, especially within the context of a U2 album at the time, in that it is merely a simple two minutes piano driven ballad. The simple, yet effective, piano patterns are complemented by a softly sung vocal performance by Bono, and the whole song works so well because it is so different to the somewhat bombastic approach towards the songs that is evident elsewhere on the album.

'*Is That All*' closes the album not with a slow burn out, which could have been anticipated, but in rage and anger, with a spirited final track. Whether lyrical ideas had temporarily run dry, or it was purely for effect is unknown, like '*Scarlet*' before it, the song took just one phrase, (as opposed to one word), and repeated it over and over again. It was a clattering semi-improvised sounding song which closed the album, a bit disappointingly.

The first side of '*October*' had hinted at better things to come than side 2 was ultimately able to deliver.

The album was, on the whole, something of a disappointment from a listening perspective after the adrenalin rushes and general exuberant naivete of '*Boy*'. The whole of the album had been completed relatively quickly, (about three months), by some standards, and all too often this was apparent on the material and songs it offered, a lot of it sounding too unfinished or incomplete.

However, '*October*' performed particularly well in the British album charts reaching Number 11, and earning the group their first silver disc in England for sales in excess of 60,000 copies.

Whilst not exactly their 'wilderness' years, it was an album both musically and lyrically that was much deeper in many ways than what they would attempt in the same way again. Perhaps suffering ultimately in the final execution as being made too soon in their careers, by a group who were still finding their feet and were still very much young and naive, and yet dealing with many deep and purposeful issues that only time can bring greater understanding and knowledge of.

'*Gloria*' was lifted as a single from the album around the time of its release, and although it had the anthem-ic quality of '*I Will Follow*', (a live version of which appeared on its b-side), it didn't make the Top 40 singles chart, lost within the excitement of the release of the album itself.

'*Gloria*' was actually the album opening track, and like '*I Will Follow*' and '*Fire*' before it, and tracks like '*New Years Day*' since, it came to epitomise the musical sounds and styles that would eventually be so readily associated with the group, as being their particular 'sound', especially around this time.

This would also eventually lead to a lot of press criticism later in their careers, being seen as responsible for turning the group into a breast-beating monster of huge proportions which many could not comprehend or tolerate.

The song had an accompanying video, (which was filmed on a barge on the waterways of Dublin), but it was not an area in which the band invested a great deal of time or effort at this point, (being before the multi-media explosion of MTV and its kind), and it would be many years before they began to look upon the visual presentation of the group themselves and the songs as being an important factor in their marketing strategies.

Following the album's release there was yet another sold out, this time consisting of an 18 dates tour of Britain; In November they went back again to play live in the US. On their return in January of 1982 they went back to Ireland to play there for the first time in over a year.

This culminated in a gig in front of 5,000 at the RDS in Dublin. It was then back on a plane to the states yet again, this time to play a number of large shows with the then hugely successful J. Geils Band.

These shows took place in large 10,000 plus capacity arenas, and although they were faced with the usual problems that a support band in this situation would encounter, lack of time for sound-checking before the gig, etc..., the shows were generally extremely well received. The crowd were demanding encores at most of the shows and U2 were quite happy to provide them so long as the J. Geils Bands crew didn't have the chance to pull the plug on them first, denying them the opportunity to potentially upstage the headliners.

Although it never appeared on an album, and was very rarely played live, the '*A Celebration*' single in October of 1982 was a powerful and aggressive representation of the sound the group were creating at the time, and which would eventually emerge more fully on the '*War*' album.

'*A Celebration*' gave the group their third consecutive minor hit single, but they were yet to reach the Top 20 of the British singles chart.

All of this frantic activity around the release of '*October*' had brought U2 all of a sudden to some sort of crisis point.

The album had drained them all both psychologically and emotionally. Bono was becoming notorious for his outspoken comments on a variety of subjects, and the touring schedule had been, for the most part, extremely intense. All in all it appeared that they might well be on the verge of splitting up. It was their manager Paul McGuiness though who eventually talked them through the turmoil.

Bono commented after the event that, *"we were being pulled in two different directions, we felt subconscious pressure being applied to us in all directions"*.

Chapter 4

## The Heart Beats Faster

During the summer of that year they had embarked on an exhausting campaign to conquer Europe, culminating with appearing at a series of festivals, and on their return to England supporting The Police at the Gateshead Stadium in the North of England .

The Autumn was spent rehearsing and writing new material. In December of '82 they played a short six date UK tour which was again a great success, selling out well in advance of the concerts, on each occasion.

On something of a roll, the band played on, the touring schedule still hectic. These shows provided the band with the first opportunity to present to their live audience the new material they had been working on, tracks that would eventually form the basis of the 'War' album.

The first taster of this third album came in the form of the single 'New Years Day'. Inspired by the Polish Solidarity movement, it was to give U2 their first bona fide hit single in Britain, reaching the Top 10 in January of 1983. It had a general up-tempo optimism about itself and was to become an important breakthrough for the group in helping to build and expand their already sizable audience.

The song's accompanying video was shot in the snow clad surroundings of the Swedish countryside, the group all looking suitably mean and moody, dressed in black, starkly illustrating the division between themselves and the virginal white of the newly fallen snow. A powerful and emotive song, Bono was lead to declare after its release and ultimate success that, *"people are growing disillusioned with pap, with the wallpaper music and gloss. It's as if someone has eaten too many smarties over the past few years, and suddenly they are beginning to feel ill as they look at the wrapping papers strewn around the room."*

On the back of this success they began yet another round of British concerts, twenty seven this time, again all sold out.

With the release of the *'War'* album in March 1983, many critics were lead to comment that it marked a new peak in the songwriting partnership of Bono and The Edge.

This was an accomplished and commercial album, again produced by Steve Lillywhite, making its debut onto the British Album charts at No.1, a week after its release. It contained some songs soon to be regarded as classics such as *'Sunday Bloody Sunday'*.

The song, written by Bono about his feelings on the political history of Northern Ireland, together with thoughts and opinions on the division within the church, proved to be a controversial opening track. It was soon to become something of an (supposedly) unintentional anthem for the group for many years to come.

In part, the song was inspired by an incident in Derry in the early 1970's, coupled with a similar one some fifty years earlier in Dublin, when British troops had fired upon innocent civilians during times of unrest. These events were still very much in the minds and thoughts of people there at the time. Many welcomed these sentiments being made known to a generally naive and misinformed world, while others thought of the past as very much gone and as such shouldn't necessarily be forgiven, but perhaps should be forgotten.

Whatever its sentiments, however, *'Sunday Bloody Sunday'* was to become something of an unintentional theme tune for U2, the same way in which a soap opera such as Dallas is very discernible by its theme tune, you hear the song and you know what programme is coming on.

'*Sunday Bloody Sunday*' the album's opener, sounds dramatically under produced on the album version of the song, coming across almost like a demo. A slightly off-key sounding electric violin was employed to bizzare effect. Sounding out of place on this album's version, it seems to have been dropped from later recordings.

The most important thing about the track for the group at the time was that it did begin to amply illustrate just what potential the group had and so showed plenty of promise for the future.

'*Sunday Bloody Sunday*' provoked a far more intense reaction from U2 fans than anything the group had experienced before.

Bono relates a story of what happened after a gig in San Francisco a couple of years later: *"I walked out of the back stage door and there were people waiting for autographs. I was given a piece of paper that was folded, and when I opened it up I realised I was about to sign my name to support some guy with Republican connections. I'd like to see a united Ireland, but I don't believe you can just put a gun to someone's head to make them see your way. Having had a Catholic mother and a Protestant father, I know how grey it is. There are no sides."*

At the end of the tour to promote the album, a second single was released. '*Two Hearts Beat As One*', reaching number 18 in the British singles chart. Remixed from the original album version for single release in the USA by dance producer Francois Kervokian, the song took on what was becoming something of a predictable U2 theme of two separate entities trying to sort out their differences.

Criticism followed this single as the group were accused of using the position they had attained to somewhat wave a white flag of peace around the world, trying to unite people together. The song did actually highlight somewhat the group's slight fragilities and self-doubts on occasion within some of their lyrical themes.

'*Two Hearts Beat As One*' was far more constructed around Adam's bass guitar sound than the Edge's often domineering guitar patterns. It is one of the album's tracks that still stands up well today, musically speaking, especially in its Kervokian constructed remix state.

Elsewhere on the '*War*' album, the group were to be found in a far more experimental frame of mind on tracks such as '*Red Light*', '*The Refugee*' and '*Surrender*'.

'*Red Light*' had a decidedly invigorating use of the trumpet writhing all through the song's middle section. This, coupled with the inspired use of Kid Creole's backing singers, The Coconuts, made for an eerie sounding U2 record, but an interestingly different one at that. In the normally expected context of a U2 record, '*Red Light*' is positively bizzare, but in its effectively executed finished state, sounds strangely appropriate.

This experimental state is continued, but with less satisfying results on '*The Refugee*', which in all honesty , is basically a rather messy song with Bono's half-spoken/half-sung vocals competing for attention with the ultimately ineffective use of a slightly African sounding drum pattern. The production of the song also sounds terribly weak, but this can be explained in part by the fact that the actual version of the song that is used on the album was the demo one. When the group had listened to the tapes of ideas of what to include on the album, they had evidently decided to retain the demo version of this song for inclusion. And so, after a bit of remix treatment by Steve Lillywhite, that is what appears. The problem this creates though is that the song has no real depth or bite about itself, even in its rough demo-state form, and so suffers as a result.

Following on from '*Sunday Bloody Sunday*', the album's second track '*Seconds*' effectively utilised a military beat to great effect. The most extraordinary departure for the group concerning '*Seconds*' however was that the lead vocal duties were not taken on by Bono this time, but instead they were tackled by The Edge, with promising results. One of the most intriguing points about The Edge's vocals on '*Seconds*' is just how similar they actually sound to Bono's.

'*Like A Song*' was, musically speaking, a bit more like the material that had been so dominant on the group's previous albums, and yet it glowed with far more confidence and determination than its predecessors. Lyrically, it found the group again reflecting on the situations that were ever dominant around them. Meaningless violence and fighting for reasons that many could not begin to comprehend. As ever the group were aware of all this and tried to put their thoughts on what was happening into the perspective of the song.

'*Drowning Man*' with its message of hope and optimism for the future was one of the albu's more musically restrained moments, and according to the group themselves one of its more effective ones. According to The Edge, this was one of the strongest tracks on the album because of the way the song had come together whilst the group were in the studio. He had said that throughout the recording of the song they each felt that they were creating something special, and went on to say that in his opinion Bono's vocal performance on the track was, up to that point, the best that he personally had ever heard him deliver.

For the track, as previously on *'Sunday Bloody Sunday'*, the group had employed the atmospheric use of an electric violin. But whereas on *'Sunday Bloody Sunday'*, it had seemed somewhat out of place and uneasy in the finished product, here it had worked to great effect, adding to the songs rich textures and complementing both Bono's vocal performance and the band's playing perfectly. It was indeed both one of the album's highlights and one of its stronger moments.

*'Surrender'* was the album's penultimate track. It chose as its lyrical theme another one of the self doubts that would creep into the band's music at the time. That being, simply the position that they held within the broad spectrum of the music business and the conflicts and tests of loyalty they would often have to endure because of it. There were also the prevalent doubts and niggles that were forever raising their heads and becoming apparent to the group, ever so often making them question their motives for carrying on.

Along with two of the albums other tracks, *'Red Light'* and *'Refugee'*, *'Surrender'* had slightly more experimental leanings on the musical side. The group were certainly beginning, by this time, to gather enough confidence within their work to, as it were, stick their necks out occasionally, and take what were for the group unknown risks.

They seemed to be making a conscious decision about their music at times to try and broaden their own horizons, at the same time as retaining the loyal and faithful following who would eagerly be anticipating their every release.

*'Surrender'* was another track that took full advantage of the use of female backing singers in order to give it a new dimension. The track has an airy, spacious feel about itself, a sound that was ultimately not dissimilar in many ways to the musical direction that they would eventually take to further heights on 1985's *'The Unforgettable Fire'*. It was certainly one of the most musically advanced songs for the group at the time.

Full use was made of The Edge's guitar work. After the previous albums simply devised three-chord structure based songs, suddenly his guitar playing took on the air of a far greater confidence and understanding toward his chosen instrument. He seemed to have made a decision to make the guitar work for him, instead of being a slave to its potential limitations.

'*Surrender*' comes across as one of the album's more confidently executed tracks. It builds and expands, creating a smooth and atmospheric presence. Bono's vocals are assured and dominant and yet they still co-exist harmoniously with the female backing singers.

'*40*', the album's closing track, was yet another spiritual evocation of the group's religious leanings, taking as it did actual words from the bible to form part of the song's lyrics. The song was soon to become the sombre and yet ultimately enthralling finale to U2's live shows at the time.

The crowd could often be heard singing the song's lyrics long after the band had left the stage, turning the song into an anthem of hope and optimism for the future, and obviously touching people in a meaningful way.

'*War*' quite aside from being what many groups discover is the 'difficult' third album, proved in many ways to a starting block towards their eventual world wide breakthrough, entering the US Top 10 and gaining them the award of their first US gold disc for sales in excess of half a million copies.

Bono was heralded as being one of the most passionately, powerful and emotive vocalists of his generation, The Edge acknowledged one of the most original and inventive guitarists, (along with the likes of Johnny Marr of The Smiths), of the decade. And Adam and Larry were credited with the honour of making the task of providing the group's rhythm section seem effortless.

The album was a great triumph for the group, more than amply highlighting their new found confidence in themselves and their material, progressing in many ways, both musically and for Bono, vocally.

With the increased popularity in America came the inevitable progression from playing clubs and the like to graduating to arenas. Indeed by the end of a three month US tour which had started in April, they had played a number of headlining gigs to over 10,000 people a night.

Although the incredible success of the album didn't exactly make them rich, (due to the large amount invested by Island in the first two albums), it was a huge and significant leap forward for the group and heralded the arrival of U2 on a global scale.

In August of 1983 the band returned to Ireland to headline 'A Day At The Races', an all day event held at Dublin's Phoenix Park. Also on the bill that day were Simple Minds and The Eurythmics, but there was little disguising the fact that most of the 25,000 strong crowd were there to welcome home and give their support to U2.

# Chapter 5

## With A Flag And Conscience

When a group becomes as big as U2, there usually grows a huge market in bootlegged material. Everything is snapped up by the ardent fan from studio out-takes, to often shabby recorded concert performances.

Hence, part of the purpose for the group's release of 'Under A Blood Red Sky' was to try and quell the ever increasing market that had arisen in U2 bootlegs.

Although they were accused of releasing a product just for the sake of it, capitalising on their ever growing live reputation, when put into perspective, 'Under A Blood Red Sky's' release was in fact justifiable.

At least it gave the fans who yearned for any live recorded material by the group they could get their hands on, (apart from some of the earlier singles b-sides), a chance to purchase something that was well recorded, packaged and had a listenable quality about it.

'*Under A Blood Red Sky*' wasn't, however, a particularly definitive representation of a U2 gig, taking as it did its eight tracks from three different concerts during the '*War*' tour in Germany, Boston and Denver. It was marketed as a mini-album and had a lower than normal retail price to reflect this.

Although the '*War*' album had effectively helped to break the group on a global scale, doing a lot of the ground work, it was also the release of '*Under A Blood Red Sky*' that helped to sustain this new found success.

Two of the album's eight tracks were taken from what was to be described as the ultimate U2 concert experience of the time at Red Rocks natural amphitheatre.

Red Rocks was chosen by the group and their manager as the perfect venue to represent and film the spectacle of a U2 show. It is a huge natural amphitheatre with a nine thousand potential capacity, ten miles outside of Denver, Colorado.

Filmed during a torrential downpour of rain, the gig was shown in full on mid-summers night on the, then, most popular music programme of the time, The Tube.

This filmed opportunity presented the group to the world raw, emotive and in full flag waving mode.

A poignant image was struck when during '*Sunday Bloody Sunday*' Bono produced a huge white flag on stage (the purpose of it being white was to represent no allegiance with anything, but to portray peace as the symbolism within, ) and pass it into the audience.

Many were critical of the seemingly blatant attempt to be some sort of spokes-people for the generation, complete with full breast-beating histrionics. The moment was strong and poignant but much maligned and misunderstood.

Ironically the live version of '*Sunday Bloody Sunday*' that found its way onto '*Under A Blood Red Sky*' was not taken from the performance at Red Rocks, but along with four of the other tracks, a version the group played at a German festival called Rockpalast '83 was used. The actual version of the song from the Rockpalast became , perhaps, the most recognisable live performance of the song that the group ever gave. This was mainly due to Bono's introduction of the song, in which he attempts to put the song into some form of context, by quelling the often thought of notions of the time as to its intent and purpose. Stating categorically that the song was not a war or rebel song and that its existence was purely devoid from these ideas or intentions.

The actual recording of the song at Rockpalast sounds slightly subdued compared with, for example, the performance given at Red Rocks, and the audience reaction and participation there, yet there was still a noticeably intense atmosphere in the air surrounding the group whenever or wherever the song is played live.

The album opened with a stirring version of *'Gloria'*. Set free from the restrictions imposed by the studio, it becomes a veritable monster of a song from the moment of Bono's introduction and The Edge's guitar bursts in with the songs familiar opening riff. The live version of *'Gloria'* is greatly aided by the ecstatic vocal presence of the crowd, singing along to every line. Another big plus is that Bono's vocals take on far more of a human quality when heard live, a slight missing of a cue, or vaguely off-key note, which would never be found on a studio version, adds rather than detracts from the finished product.

Indeed, with this semi-improvised feel occurring on a lot of the material, the group's versions of, particularly popular songs, takes on a different meaning, and it becomes quite a frustrating dilemma to merely hear the song, when it would be a far more enjoyable and advantageous proposition to actually be able to see what the group, and Bono in particular, are doing during key moments in a songs performance. Of course a live album is a testament and record of a show but it cannot ultimately represent the feeling of actually being there, and experiencing it first hand. This problem is occasionally apparent with *'Under A Blood Red Sky'*. The album lacks a certain amount of continuity due to the fact that the tracks are taken from three different concerts. Whereas, for example, the generally accepted accompanying video to this project, the *'Under A Blood Red Sky'* live video, takes as its subject matter and content, just the groups performance at Red Rocks in Colorado. The only two surviving tracks from Red Rocks were, the aforementioned *'Gloria'* and *'Party Girl'*. Apart from the five recorded at the German Rockpalast festival, the album's only other track *'11 O'clock, Tick Tock'*, was taken from a show the group played in Boston during the previous American tour.

*'11 O'Clock, Tick, Tock'*, the non album featured single from the Boston concert had a much more laid back sound for the group than elsewhere on the album, and although it is equally as well received by the crowd as the other tracks it is not one of the live highlights, sounding as it does to withdrawn and lacklustre for a U2 concert.

The *'Boy'* album's *'I Will Follow'* is given a faithful and enthusiastic delivery by the group, and accordingly given a good reception by the crowd.

Also from the *'Boy'* album, *'The Electric Co'* is featured. Significantly, only the more melodic and approachable *'Gloria'* had been used from the generally inaccessible and confused *'October'* album.

*'Party Girl'*, the other track taken from the Red Rocks show becomes a huge audience participation number for the crowd, their spirits obviously high despite the horrendous weather on the night of the Red Rocks show, they are left to finish the song off on the band's behalf once they had stopped playing and singing.

*'Under A Blood Red Sky'* closes in fine form with the instantly recognisable *'New Years Day'* single from the *'War'* album and the familiar closing song to their shows at the time, *'40'*.

The performance or perhaps, rather recording, of *'New Years Day'* seems somewhat muted and restrained compared to the previous tracks. Whilst *'40'* is straightforward and remains pretty much faithful to the *'War'* album version. That is, up until the end however when the group stops playing and leaves the task of finishing of both the song and the album in the more than capable hands of the fans, who of course know every word and carry the song to its climax.

*'Under A Blood Red Sky'* is a competent example of the sort of shows and performances that the group were giving around that time without necessarily being an earth shattering or stunning display of new potential. It returns ultimately to the problem that to really appreciate a live U2 show, one has to be there, although of course, records such as *'Under A Blood Red Sky'* can at least preserve the memory of the moment, and give the listener the chance to relive those memories over and over again. For this reason alone its release is ultimately necessary and justifiable.

At the end of November the group set off for the Far East and Japan to play their first live concerts there.

A triumphant return in January of 1984 saw them awarded with a platinum disc for sales of *'Under A blood Red Sky'*, and at the same time the *'War'* album notched up its twelfth consecutive month on the UK album charts.

In march of 1984 yet another honour was bestowed upon them when the readers of Rolling Stone magazine voted them as their band of the year for 1983, on the strength of the *'War'* album.

By the end of the 1980's this had escalated to band of the decade, again awarded by the readers of Rolling Stone.

# Chapter 6

## The Fire Burns Brighter

During the next few months whilst recording and writing their next album at Dublin's Windmill studios with Brian Eno and Daniel Lanois, Paul McGuiness re-negociated a new deal for the band with Island Records which proved to be far more beneficial to the group than their original one.

Under their previous deal they received a reasonably small advance on albums, for recording costs etc, and by many standards a fairly modest royalty rate on sales.

The new deal was very shrewdly conducted and reflected very much their new found status and success within the music industry. It gave them a guaranteed $2 million dollar advance per album, plus approximately double their previous royalty rate. This pretty much guaranteed that whatever happened they would all now be financially secure for life.

The new deal also gave them many other benefits from being able to chose their own producer for future work, to being able to present to Island any new material they recorded without any interference or particular input from Island. Effectively this meant that any material they were to write and produce, Island would have to have enough faith to release it onto the market, without any questions asked.

Any reservations that avant-garde performer and producer Brian Eno may have had about working with U2 seemed non-founded when the first fruits of the U2/Eno/Lanois collaborations emerged in the shape of *'Pride (In The Name Of Love)*, the first single from *'The Unforgettable Fire'* album.

*'Pride'* was U2's first single release in over a year and was soon to become their biggest hit single to date, reaching Number 3 in the charts and earning themselves their first silver disc in the UK for singles sales. The earlier worries of the group being an albums and not particularly a singles band were now looking unfounded.

Dedicated to civil rights leader Martin Luther King, *'Pride'* was by far their most accomplished release to date and although the group felt it could actually give them a Number One single reaching Number Three was a great achievement. Its release granted U2 new respect and admiration from both critics and the public alike. Bono's vocal performance on the single took on new highs, delivering an emotive and blistering strength.

In August of 1984 they set off on a world tour of which the first six weeks were spent playing shows in New Zealand and Australia. Attendance and public support were phenomenal with the group playing to over 60,000 people attending the group's five shows in Sydney and over 30,000 turning up at Melbourne.

When the Australasian leg of the tour finished at the end of September, the interest generated by these shows had meant that they had four albums in the Australian charts and the *'Pride'* single had risen to a creditable Number Four.

However, by the group's own admission, they had set themselves up with incredibly high standards and they felt that the shows themselves on this leg of the tour were not in fact, musically, a huge success.

The, at times, orchestrated feel to parts of the new material of *'Unforgettable fire'* proved very difficult to reproduce live. So at the end of this six weeks jaunt they returned to Dublin to rethink the new shows' format, for subsequent performances in Europe and the States.

The album they were touring to promote, *'The Unforgettable Fire'* was released worldwide in October of 1984; it instantly crashed into the British Album charts at Number One.

The album possessed on the whole a much more lush sound than anything which had preceded it.

This album was a slightly different departure for Brian Eno who was better known firstly as a founder member of Roxy Music in the early 1970's and secondly for his pioneering work in the field of ambient music.

The other main contributor to the production work and sound on the album was Canadian Daniel Lanois, a much respected sound engineer at the time, who would continue to work with the group for some years to come after the album.

*'The Unforgettable Fire'* was a definite departure from the previous powerful and aggressive *'War'* and *'Blood Red Sky'* albums. Utilising Eno's guidance and influence well to create an at times sparser and more ambient feel to the sound. Gently coaxing the listener in rather than the previous method of attacking them head on.

The album took its title from a book which was also an exhibition showing a series of paintings and drawings of survivors of the Hiroshima/Nagasaki atomic bomb.

These images were the primary inspiration for the album's mesmerising title track. With its orchestrated feel, using a string arrangement to great effect, the song had a smooth seductive dreamlike quality about it.

The *'Unforgettable Fire'* single was one of the many U2 tracks that really came alive and benefited when given the remix treatment so common when a track is lifted from an album for single release. The single still sounds stunning today when heard on the radio in its remixed form. The album's version was in itself good but when remixed it takes on a whole new life, the remixes having turned the song into a musical soundscape of epic proportions and grandeur.

Part of the problem when making a record sound as good as this however, is that it becomes nearly impossible to recreate the same sound as had been achieved on record, live. This was one of the songs that would prove to be near to impossible to accurately recreate when played live in concert.

The same problem was to occur with *'Wire'*, which although retaining much of the feel of the band's earlier material, had a new dimension added to it by its use of a sequencer, adding a far more complex sound to the overall result. The same could again be said of *'Indian Summer Sky'*, the song worked, but only up to a point.

The influence of the band's travels, particularly in America began to show through on much of the new material. One of the tracks to determinedly show this was also ironically one of the album's weaker moments, *'Elvis Presley And America'*. This had a plodding, undetermined and dysfunctional feel to itself, the vocals were not clear, the lyrics somewhat confusing and obscure and the music sounding unsatisfyingly incomplete. The track shuffled along without appearing to head or reach anywhere in particular. This was a classic case of an excellent song title, which held so much promise, disguising what was in fact a poor and disappointing song.

A couple of other tracks also failed to hit the required mark such as *'Promenade'* and the meandering guitar piece, *'4th Of July'*. They were both pleasant enough but came across as being little more than adequate and routine album fillers.

The next track on the album was the undeniably excellent *'Bad'*, the song that would eventually help to propel the group towards their present day status through its performance during 'Live Aid'.

*'Bad'*, with its slowly building layers of sound became, and indeed still is today, an integral part of their live performances. It's a song that just screams out to be played live and consequently the recorded version does suffer slightly due to its being performed in a sterile studio setting.

The album closes with the semi accapella, beautiful lullaby feel of *'MLK'*, quite a relief after the discordant dablings of *'Elvis Presley And America'*, and a prime example of the fact that simplicity when constructing a song is often a far greater weapon than hurling bucket loads of the studios technological artillery at it.

From a personal perspective, listening to *'The Unforgettable Fire'* after experiencing the exhilaration of *'Boy'*, the album appears in many places to be too preoccupied and swamped in unnecessary extravagance to be regarded as a complete success. It's almost as if in places sound effects and ideas were thrown in for the mere sake that they existed, and were at the group's disposal, and so should be used.

The album's general departure from previous sounding material had been something of a risk to undertake for the group, they nearly left the whole project unrecorded in the early stages, worried somewhat by the great leap forward that they were taking which would put them in previously unknown territory.

However, despite one or two not wholeheartedly encouraging reviews, particularly in America, this departure proved to be a more than satisfying success for the group in many ways. Bono said some years later that it was on *'The Unforgettable Fire'* album that he *"first learnt to sing"*.

*'Unforgettable Fire'* was widely thought of as being the album that would break them into the American market in a big way, with the *'Pride'* single leading the assault. But although the single was to make significant in-roads for the group, spending fifteen weeks and reaching Number 33 on the Billboard singles chart, the album wasn't the immediate success that they'd anticipated and hoped for.

Although it did gradually receive huge support particularly on US college radio, which in time was to help it on its way to become the group's first American million seller, for which they were presented with a platinum disc.

They were also aided, as many before them and certainly since, by the enormous support given to the *'Pride'* single by 24 hour music station MTV, who were regularly airing the video.

MTV also showed a half hour documentary style presentation of the making of the *'Unforgettable Fire'* album. This was later to reappear on the *'Unforgettable Fire'* video collection along with promotional videos for some of the earlier singles. This collection was released in the UK in October of 1985.

Chapter 7


# A New Found Confidence


In November of 1984 they played their first British concerts in over 18 months, which included two of their biggest so far, playing at the Wembley Arena in London for two nights.

The touring continued in the States in December with a short series of concerts on the East Coast. These were intended as a warm up exercise for a proposed larger and more advertised visit the following Spring.

This two week excursion saw them easily sell out in the 3-5,000 seat venues they were booked to play. They could have sold out in much larger venues, which was reflected by the short visit's final two concerts on the west coast. These included playing at the Long Beach Arena in Los Angeles which has a capacity of over 12,000.

After returning to spend Christmas at home, they then went off for a tour of European countries in January of 1985.

This more than adequately set them up for their biggest assault on America yet, which began in Dallas, Texas on February 25th, 1985, the start of a tour which would take them through until the beginning of May.

The interest and support they were now generating was enough to not only take *'Unforgettable Fire'* through the million seller mark but also see the sales figures for *'War'* doubled, again giving them a platinum disc for million plus sales. *'Under A blood Red Sky'* was also still performing well, with half a million copies sold in February '85, this had again cruised past the million mark by Summer of that same year.

The new American shows were beginning to take on a new meaning for the group with the audience growing all the time.

Not just established U2 fans were turning up but others who had either heard about the group first hand or had read the ecstatic reviews were also attending the shows.

The shows themselves were an exquisite mixture of the best moments from the first four albums, coupled with some novel interpretations of favourite songs; snatches of Bob Dylan's *'Knockin' on Heaven's Door'*, The Rolling Stones' *'Ruby Tuesday'* or the Beatles *'Dear Prudence'* would be added to instrumental parts of various songs, giving them a different meaning or showing them up in a new light.

The band's new found confidence and maturity was shinning through.

Despite the transition to bigger crowds there was still a form of intimacy in their performances which had previously worked so well in the smaller clubs.

The need to progress on to playing larger arenas was inevitable. The band had no problem selling tickets wherever they played, in fact demand was so great that to have stayed on a smaller level would have deprived their audience of the chance to see them. This had been amply illustrated by the December tour when touts had been able to charge anything up to $150 for a single ticket.

Despite reservations about the move to larger arenas, the band had conceded that they were a big group, could make the larger places work for rather than against them and that the progression was necessary in order to accommodate the fans.

This meant that a bigger and tighter operation was required all round. Security was always a problem in one way or another, with various members of the audience determined in their quest to touch or simply be on stage in the presence of their heroes. These lucky few who penetrated the by now routine security barriers that surrounded the stage were not just instantly bundled off to the sides to be ejected from the building as is often the case, but were treated with a degree of respect and dignity. They were 'escorted' off and let back into the crowd at a more strategic position.

The American tour reached a new peak of achievement on April 1st when the group played at Madison Square Garden in New York for the first time.

Playing there is generally thought of as being an achievement for any group and it was a particularly poignant land mark for U2.

Despite the fact that they had already and were still to play larger venues, performing at Madison Square was the sure fire way of the band themselves knowing that they had actually made it as big as everyone said they were.

To mark this momentous occasion they flew in from Ireland many friends, family and Irish journalists at their own cost who were presented with the best seats in the house in order to witness just what a progression the four lads from Mount Temple had made.

By the end of the tour on the 4th May, U2 had played to over half a million people, had been pronounced Band Of the 80's by Rolling Stone magazine and had four of their five albums on the American Billboard chart.

In April the title track of 'Unforgettable Fire' was released as a UK single entering the chart a week after its release at Number 8. As a bonus for the fans it was released with the addition of previously unavailable tracks making up the 12" and double pack versions b-sides, plus a live recording of 'A Sort Of Homecoming' on the reverse of the 7".

Also widely available around this time but not granted an official British release until 1987 was the 4 track EP 'Wide Awake In America'.

Intended at first only for the US market, it became a huge seller on import in Britain mainly due to its inclusion of what many regarded as the definitive live version of the big crowd favourite 'Bad'.

In June they played their only British date that summer at the Milton Keynes Bowl and a week later had returned to Ireland to play a triumphant home coming gig for over 55,000 fans in Dublin's Croke Park.

On the 13th July, 1985, two weeks after Croke Park, U2 went to Wembley Stadium in London to play at the historic Live Aid concert.

# Chapter 8

# The World Watched Too

Live Aid was performed on the back of the success attained by the '*Do They Know It's Christmas/Feed The World*' single by a large group of successful musicians at the time, collectively known as Band Aid.

The initial inspiration for the Band Aid single was prompted when Irishman Bob Geldof was sitting at home one evening, watching the television, and a four minutes film report came on during the news from Ethiopia about a large scale famine many parts of that country was enduring.

As a small way of helping, he decided to make a record to raise money for famine relief. Along with Midge Ure of Ultraxox he wrote the song '*Do They Know Its Christmas*', which was recorded in late November 1984. Together with over forty other musicians,

Bono and Adam from U2 had attended and contributed to the recording.

Fuelled by the global success of the single which became the UK's biggest ever selling single and raised well over £8 million worldwide the next obvious step to Geldof and the newly formed Band Aid organisation was to take the proceedings one step further. They decided to stage a concert hopefully attracting as big stars as the single had done and try to raise yet more money and create awareness toward the problem.

The plan was for there to be two simultaneous 'Live Aid' concerts taking place some 3,000 miles apart, one in Wembley Stadium, England the other at the John F Kennedy Stadium in Philadelphia, USA.

These were to form a carefully co-ordinated programme of which each act at Wembley Stadium was allocated an approximate twenty minute slot. There was a total of 63 different acts performing in both London and Philadelphia with a potential world wide audience of at least 80% of the total number of television sets in existence in the world, or equalling a potential world wide audience of over one billion viewers.

U2 were in Manchester, England finishing off a year long British and European tour when the call came in from Bob Geldof asking the band if they would play at the British end of Live Aid.

Despite having been on the road solidly for a year and badly being in need of a rest, the band had no hesitation in agreeing to pledge their support and contribute to the day's live entertainment. *"It was something we had to do, I just couldn't say no"*, said Bono after taking Geldof's call.

U2 took to the Wembley stage to an encouraging reception some time after 5 o'clock in the afternoon, just when the crowd needed a lift after the subdued performances given by Bryan Ferry and Paul Young.

They crashed straight into *'Sunday Bloody Sunday'*. Many fans at the gig appeared to be there specifically to see U2 as home-made banners supporting the group were suddenly visible in the sea of people. The sound at first seemed far from perfect but the rousing anthem of *'Sunday'* was enough to get the crowd on their feet and moving, giving the afternoon the lift and boost that was sorely needed.

*'Sunday Bloody Sunday'* finished with much cheering and applause, then with the words *"we're an Irish band, we come from Dublin City Ireland, like all cities it has it's good and it has it's bad. This is a song called 'Bad'."*, they were to go through a fifteen minute

period which was to unknowingly present the group to the world on a larger scale than ever before and which was to ultimately help to shape and form a path for the next phase of their careers.

The intention had been to play three songs that day but *'Bad'* became an extended performance taking in many facets along the way. Near the end of the song it became a huge audience participation number taking in snatches of The Rolling Stones *'Ruby Tuesday'* and a line from *'Sympathy For The Devil'* to the chorus from Lou Reed's *'Walk On The Wild Side'*, where the lyrics from *'Holly's'* trek across America to take in a stop in London Town at Wembley Stadium, much to the audience's obvious delight.

The most moving and poignant part of this performance however was to occur when Bono took an impromptu 'walkabout' during an instrumental part of the song. He gazed into the audience and seemed to become aware of the problems security were having with the crush of people at the front. He vigorously pointed out whom to remove to give some breathing space.

Then, in what appeared at first to be a moment of madness and stupidity but was to turn out remarkably different, he flung himself off the front of the stage down into the security pit, to lend some assistance. Arms instantly stretched at the front to try and touch him but he had fixed his gaze on a young girl, still stuck in the crowd at the front, wearing a white top. He pointed her out to security and then helped to prise her from the assembled throng. Then as a reward for her persistence, he embraced and then indulged in a moment of slow dancing with her.

A perfect moment and indeed photo opportunity was instantly created of Bono dancing with this dark haired young girl who was obviously so overcome with what was happening to her that you could see the tears in her eyes.

Back near the front of the stage two more young women from the audience were offered heartfelt embraces and kisses as well.

Then after improvising the end of the song he left the crowd with the words *"thank you and God bless you"*, picked up a white towel, waved and departed the stage.

What could have been a self indulgent performance, had in fact been a spontaneous, riveting and moving one.

Although it was generally felt that Queen stole the show that day with their impeccably constructed greatest hits set, U2 were one of the groups that ran them a close second, helping to make the day a remarkable and poignant one. Their performance was to be a magnificent way to finish off the Unforgettable Fire tour.

After the triumph of Live Aid the band members took a three

months break from their own touring and recording commitments, reassembling again as a unit in November of 1985.

# Chapter 9

## A Helping Hand

During this break from each other they were all far from being idle.

The Edge worked with Jah Wobble on his 'Invaders Of The Earth' ambient dance project. Bono, after spending some five weeks with wife Ali in Africa, returned to contribute to a number of different projects including a duet with Clannad on their 'In A Lifetime' single and spending some time in New York meeting two of his idols, Mick Jagger and Keith Richards.

Whilst in New York he also contributed to the Artists Against Apartheid movement, fronted by former Bruce Springsteen guitarist Steven Van Zandt. He sang on and took part in the 'Sun City' video and single and contributed the uncredited bluesy sounding 'Silver And Gold' to the projects album.

In November of 1985 the band came back together again

fresher and bristling with ideas after their much needed break from each other.

They initially met up again at Larry's new home near the sea at Howth in Ireland to discuss and formulate ideas, with the plan being to move on to Adam's house Danesmoate at Rathfarnham where major sound and recording decisions would be made.

Over the next few months ideas were formulated, these always started from scratch with short phrases or chord sequences in mind, which were never fully completed but would evolve themselves into songs whilst they were in the studio, gradually taking a definite form and structure.

Whilst this was happening honours and critical acclaim were still very much forthcoming. In February of 1986 they swept the board at the Rolling Stone magazine's influential readers poll, including sharing the top live entertainment award with the doyen of the stadium circuit Bruce Springsteen.

Then, in May they headlined 'Self Aid' an event at Dublin's Croake Park designed to bring attention and awareness to the unemployed of Ireland and to benefit them in some way.

Many of Ireland's top groups and artists of the time were assembled, including Van Morrison, The BoomTown Rats and Chris De Burgh, with a crowd of some thirty thousand anticipated to attend on the night.

'Self Aid' went off despite a lot of savage criticism in Dublin's local press at the time, that the event was in a way allowing the somewhat negligent Irish government to disguise the problems that were existing in Ireland, by ably supporting and helping to stage the benefit, but in reality doing very little to solve the problems that existed. Bono struck back at the critics with a lyrical attack whilst on stage during the night of the concert.

The band's set that night encompassed their own standard live favourites such as *'Bad'* and *'Pride...'* along with cover versions of such crowd pleasers as Eddie Cochran's *'C'mon Everybody'* and more poignant choices like Bob Dylan's *'Maggie's Farm'*, which was delivered in such a way as to be a far more effective way of expressing their feelings that night than making an impassioned and rehearsed speech ever could.

In August of 1985 U2 had pledged their support to Amnesty International when the band's manager Paul McGuiness had been approached in Dublin by the organisation's American director Jack Healey, with a request asking if the band would consider taking part in a two week trek through some of America's major cities, as part of what was to be known as the 'Conspiracy Of Hope' tour, commemorating Amnesty's twenty fifth year in existence.

The group were keen to pledge their support, having already played a concert at New York's Radio City Music Hall during the last tour, the proceeds of which went to Amnesty.

Their appearance at Croake Park's 'Self Aid' was an ideal way of running through, with the benefit of a live audience, what was to become their thirty minute set for the 'Conspiracy Of Hope' concerts.

None of the new material that they had been working on in Dublin was yet ready for a public airing and so the chosen covers were an ideal way of presenting a different facet of the band to the crowds, along with playing the afore mentioned crowd favourites.

'The Conspiracy Of Hope' tour was to culminate at the Giants Stadium in New York on June 15th, having kicked off in San Francisco on June 4th, taking in stops at Los Angeles, Denver, Chicago and Atlanta along the way.

Apart from U2 the bill also included Lou Reed, Jackson Browne, Joan Baez, Bryan Adams and among others, Sting, who was set to reform The Police in Atlanta for the concerts there and in New York.

There were also to be many other celebrities and artists appearing at selected shows along the way, participating and offering their support in their own ways.

The purpose of the 'Conspiracy Of Hope' tour was not just to raise money, but to try and encourage young Americans to become aware and help campaign for the release of the many thousands of political prisoners languishing in the world's jails, unable to receive anything in the form of a 'fair trial'.

People at the concerts were actively encouraged to write letters of protest and concern to the relevant heads of state expressing their feelings on the situation, and hopefully benefiting in some way many of those that Amnesty sought to help.

The Amnesty tour was not only successful in its thought provoking aims but proved to be a big financial hit as well, raising some three to four million dollars worth of aid for the Amnesty organisation, helping them to continue with their work.

Taking part in Amnesty was also to be something of an unintentional master-stroke for U2 as well.

Although they were by no means at the time in the legend class of some of their contemporaries on the tour, it gave them a huge amount of publicity and access through the American media into previously uncharted territories, such as the huge expanse of 'mid-America'. The publicity the tour gave them, along with their well received performances led to a huge rise in record sales of their previously released products, many stores allocating the group large displays of the previous albums and reported sales figures rose as a result, to double anything they had previously experienced with the group.

Shortly after returning from the Amnesty tour the group suffered a major loss when an important member of their road crew was tragically killed in a motorcycle accident.

Greg Carroll had been, as many of those who worked around them were, not just a member of their personal staff, mainly looking after Bono, but a friend as well.

As a tribute to Greg Carroll, the group's next album 'The Joshua Tree' was dedicated to him.

# Chapter 10

## A Nation Beckons

The progression from 'Unforgettable Fire' to 'The Joshua Tree' was gradual in parts but was certainly a very definite and intentional one.

The *Unforgettable Fire's* breathy landscapes of sound were replaced with a more confident, generally American influenced sounding result. Lyrically they were beginning to portray thoughts and ideas in a much more direct and yet meaningful way. America became a dominant inspiration for many of the lyrical themes, particularly *'Bullet The Blue Sky'* *'In Gods Country'* and *'Red Hill Mining Town'*.

The problem of heroin addiction was observed and tackled thoughtfully on *'Running To Stand Still'*, inspired by the problem becoming prevalent on their very own doorsteps on the streets of Dublin.

'*The Joshua Tree*' was to become a slightly rare commodity for the group, given that two of its tracks were to eventually be covered for single releases by other artists. The Pet Shop Boys were first off the mark incorporating their own uniquely interesting version of '*Where The Streets Have No Name*' into one of their singles, sequining the song with another cover of the camp disco anthem '*Can't Take My Eyes Off You*'. Then British Soul group The Chimes covered and had a Top 10 hit with their own version of '*I Still Haven't Found What I'm Looking For*', a song that U2 also scored a Top 10 hit in Britain and a number 1 with in America themselves.

The visual presentation and packaging of the album also took a new direction for the group. '*The Joshua Tree*' appeared more glossy and lavishly packaged than any of its predecessors, and also somewhat more self assured. Significantly, perhaps, for the first time all the song's lyrics were reproduced on the album's inner sleeve. The photography used for the cover and inside shots were also different, utilising the talents of renowned photographer Anton Corbin to great effect. He has taken most of the groups more visually exciting photographs since and has also been instrumental in photographing and helping to present Depeche Mode's live concerts, with a series of striking images and pictures.

The albums release was preceded by the single '*With Or Without You*'. Whilst not perhaps being one of the albums most obviously commercial tracks, it was however the ideal release to show the progression the band were making from the previous album. It retained some of the smooth and sophisticated hallmarks that were apparent on '*Unforgettable Fire*', particularly the title track, yet ideally led the way for what to expect from the new material.

'*With Or Without You*' peaked at a very respectable Number 4 in the English charts but perhaps far more significantly it was to give the group their first Number 1 single in America, climbing to the summit of the charts some eight weeks after its release there.

This achievement was greatly helped by Islands marketing and promotion people having learnt a valuable lesson over what had hindered previous American single releases for the group, such as in the case of '*Pride*', where its release there was some weeks behind that of England and the rest of Europe.

This had therefore afforded ample opportunity for American record stores to be flooded with import copies and so hamper the singles American release, ( of singles like '*Pride*'), with regard to chart positions and indeed sales.

The album itself also succeeded magnificently, topping the charts not just in Britain and America but also in pretty much every other major record buying territory in the world in which it was released.

The album opened with the now familiar slowly building and then explosive force of one of its future single releases '*Where The Streets Have No Name*'. The next two tracks were again within the recognisable singles territory, '*I Still Haven't Found What I'm Looking For*', and '*With Or Without You*', until track four, and what was to become one of the future highlights, and still remains so today, whenever they played live, '*Bullet The Blue Sky*'.

Story-telling within the lyrical content of their songs was a large feature of much of '*The Joshua Tree's*' material, particularly with songs like '*Bullet The Blue Sky*'. A moody and haunting song, '*Bullet The Blue Sky's*' strength also lay in Bono's half-spoken, half-growled vocal delivery, both authoritative and atmospheric at the same time. They were, however, also able to show enough small touches of vulnerability to give the song an extra edge.

Despite its lyrical content, dealing with the heroin problem on their own doorsteps on the streets of Dublin, '*Running To Stand Still*' has that American feel which particularly dominates the album's instrumentation. The opening guitar twang evokes images in keeping with the album's cover shots of deserts and deserted ramshackle ghost towns, long forgotten in the middle of Americas sprawling metropolis elsewhere.

There must have been many debates and musings over which tracks would be lifted for single release merely due to the abundance of possibilities on offer.

One of the tracks that wasn't afforded a single release but could very comfortably have been, was '*Red Hill Mining Town*'. Building verses make way for impossibly perfect sing-a-long style choruses, and this coupled with Bono's heart wrenched vocals make '*Red Hill Mining Town*' one of the undoubted highlights of '*The Joshua Tree*'. Incidentally, '*Red Hill Mining Town*' was rarely, if ever, played live in concert by the group, the reason for this being that Bono complained that the high pitch he had chosen to deliver the vocal in on the album was very difficult for him to reproduce live, and when he tried he found that it gave him throat problems. This had also presented problems and hampered the initial plans by the record company to issue '*Red Hill Mining Town*' as the follow-up single to '*With Or Without You*'.

Another song on the album with immense commercial appeal, and one that was indeed released as a single in America, but not in Britain, was '*In Gods Country*'. It surprisingly failed to make the Top 40 of the Billboard singles chart in America, although this could perhaps be put down in part to its having no accompanying promotional video, an essential, particularly in America. Its release also came some time after that of the album itself, and by that stage 'Joshua Tree' had already sold an enormous quantity in America, and so demand for a new single from the album wasn't particularly there. It was, however, another track from the album that had the words 'single' subconsciously written all over it, and so its release was not a huge surprise.

Although it was not released officially as a single in Britain, it did however reach number 48 in the singles chart due to the large number of import copies sold which had been brought into the country from America.

This actually highlighted the group's wide spread appeal immensely as the single did not actually contain any previously unreleased tracks not available before to the British public, as perhaps could be expected. Instead the two other tracks were previously available on the 'Joshua Tree' album, straight versions of 'Running To Stand Still' and 'Bullet The Blue Sky'.

'Trip Through Your Wires' was one of the album's more noticeably American influenced tracks, along with the aforementioned ones such as 'Red Hill Mining Town'. 'Trip Through Your Wires' again had a very commercial sound, employing the use of an harmonica to good effect. Although, perhaps it should be said that the harmonica is a much over used musical instrument whenever groups or artists feel the need to inject some sort of roots or gutsy feel into their music.

'Mothers Of The Disappeared', the album's closing track was somewhat similar in style to the way they had closed the previous 'War' and 'Unforgettable Fire' albums with '40' and 'MLK' respectively. As with the previous songs it was a simply executed and yet gentle and poignant finale.

'The Joshua Tree', with its lyricisms drawing heavily on American influences, brought on in part by the vast amounts of time they were spending there, and observations they were making due to this, was the album the group needed to really establish itself in a big and challenging way there.

It was a big break, not just in the cosmopolitan capitals of New York and the West Coast areas, but also in the more difficult to conquer areas of 'Mid America', a huge territory of potential converts to their music and subsequent record buyers of the future.

The album, which was named after the Californian town where Country star Gram Parsons had died, had within its songs both a mixture of commercial appeal with 'I Still Haven't Found What I'm

*Looking For'*, alongside more experimental numbers like *'One Tree Hill'*, a song named after one of the largest mountains in New Zealand overlooking the harbour in Auckland. As a mark of respect and by way of tribute for the sadly missed Greg Carroll, who was of Maori descent, *'One Tree Hill'* was later released as a single in both New Zealand and Australia.

The world wide achievement and acclaim the band were afforded by the success of *'The Joshua Tree'* album was poignantly illustrated in April of 1987, when they became only the third band in history (the previous having been The Beatles and The Who) to be featured on the cover of the prestigious Time magazine.

In May a second single was lifted for release from the album. *'I Still Haven't Found What I'm Looking For'* reached Number 6 in the UK but more impressively gave them their second consecutive Number 1 single in America.

The song was in its own way seemingly effortless and indeed the most commercial sounding song on the album. Yet its lyrical messages of spiritual and emotional yearning was to set it aside somewhat from the trivial sounding norm of its contemporaries.

The video for the song, shot in Las Vegas caught the band in semi-busking mode, simple and yet effective.

Most of the footage was shot outside the gambling capital of America's imposing casinos and gaudy theatres, a scenario the group certainly didn't appear to identify with or yearn for.

The album received not just universal praise in its reviews but merited special occasions taking place upon its release.

Tower Records in London stayed open well into the early hours of the morning specifically for the record's release, putting the album on sale on the stroke of midnight, generating long queues, safe in the knowledge that this marketing exercise would create huge crowds and sales to the store.

*'The Joshua Tree'* marked U2's unequivocal arrival at a new peak in their careers. They had produced an album of immense promise that amply illustrated a new found maturity and confidence in their musical growth, and one which they would now be able to build from. The only real question left for the group after the success of *'The Joshua Tree'* was where would they go from here.

# Chapter 11


## Holding Up The Traffic


Upon the album's release the group had begun rehearsing the new material for a mammoth world tour which would include their first full scale American concerts for over two years.

The success of both the album and its singles meant that they had reached something of a new plateau of achievement. The shows they were undertaking were now becoming more than just concerts but had graduated into full scale events.

The band were now comfortably able to fill the 20,000+ arenas and sport stadiums amply, illustrated by the tour's first two American dates at the beginning of April which took place at the 13,500 capacity Temple State University stadium in Arizona.

The shows had huge pulling power, creating a field day for the ticket touts who were often comfortably able to charge upwards of a hundred dollars for a fifteen dollars ticket.

By the time the tour had hit Connecticut in the first week of May they had achieved not only a Number 1 single (*'With Or Without You'*) but the album was also sitting proudly on top of the Billboard album charts, an impressive feat, and even more so when it is achieved, as U2 did, simultaneously.

The album's general success in America was partly due to the policy of many radio stations there of not just playing commercially released singles but heavily featuring album tracks as well. In this way the listener was offered the opportunity to brace the whole spectrum of an artist's / band's work and not just whatever the record company was trying to push or what they would see with an accompanying video, which would often detract from the song, on MTV or such like.

All this incredible success, whilst welcomed and cherished by the band, bought along with it many unexpected and unwanted offers and hassles, that if allowed would soon be clogging up their everyday lives.

Many offers of corporate sponsorship were presented to the band, offering huge financial rewards in return for lending the group's name to their products, soft drinks, beer producers, etc...

All however were strongly declined, whatever temptations were provocatively dangled in front of their faces. When a company even offered to donate a large amount of money to a charity of the group's choice in return for their signature, this was also turned down. The group in fact suggested to the manufacturers that they could still make a worthwhile and appreciated donation quietly and simply, without having to have the group's faces behind their products to achieve this.

The Edge did comment that the group had yet to find a beer that they liked enough to want to endorse, but the message was clearly spelt out that U2 and corporate sponsorship did not equate.

The U2 phenomenon and reputation was now even preceding themselves, spreading far and wide.

Many who had overcome serious illness or self induced states of deterioration would readily credit the band or particularly Bono as being instrumental in some way towards their recovery.

Fans were regularly travelling from all corners of the world to meet and stand outside the various band members' houses, hoping either for a glimpse of their heroes or indeed anyone they could readily associate with the band.

Photo opportunities by all and sundry were seized upon often with improbable results, Bono quipped, *"You get someone with their arm around you for a photograph and the next thing you know you get a paternity suit."*

'*Where The Streets Have No Name*' was the third single from the '*Joshua Tree*' album. Memorable not just for being an ideal opening track for the album with its pulsating, driving beat, but even more so when released as a single for its accompanying video.

Shot in true Beatles 'on the roof-top' style, not in London as they had done (for inclusion in the 1967 film *Let It Be)*, but in downtown Los Angeles.

The filming of the video made widespread local and national news in America and for good reason.

Many local radio stations had become aware of U2's intention to film the video and in their wisdom had broadcast to their listeners over the air not only the location, but more significantly which band it was who would be filming there that afternoon.

Widespread chaos seemed on the cards when hundreds of fans besieged the filmings location. As the crowds got bigger and traffic was brought to a virtual standstill the police arrived on the scene.

However no trouble ensued and the afternoons events were perfectly captured and illustrated on the single's accompanying video.

"*Rock 'n' Roll music held up the city, stopped the traffic*" commented Bono in a later radio station interview and he was right.

The interest the filming of the video provoked helped the single follow its predecessors straight up the Billboard Top 100 singles chart.

By the end of the year *The 'Joshua Tree'* had topped the album charts of over 20 countries and notched up an immensely impressive sales tally of over 12 million copies sold world wide.

The latter part of 1987 was spent touring America, with the significant factor in this being, that this time they were beginning to include stadium dates alongside the customary arena ones.

This transition was not actually a great problem for the band, as they had previously taken on and conquered such challenges before, as in the cases of playing Dublin's Croake Park and at Live Aid. The band's main argument to themselves for playing these huge shows, was that they were making such big music that it demanded a big setting and that they weren't very good at playing in the small clubs anyway.

The shows were a mixture of the familiar arena ones, with stadiums tackled where the potential to fill them was justified. This meant stadium shows in areas like Boston and Philadelphia, which proved to be one of the tour's highlights, when the band were joined on stage by Bruce Springsteen for a couple of numbers.

Chapter 12

## A Vision Shared

The next few months were spent in a seemingly endless round of 'meet-and-greet' style appearances and contributions to other projects.

This started with the band recording *'Its Christmas' (Baby Please Come Home)*, a Phil Spector song originally recorded by Darlene Love for inclusion on a various artists charity album, *'A Very Special Christmas'*. Sticking very much to the original sound and even having Darlene Love sing backing vocals the track was a fine testament to the claim that the group were no longer in fact the world's worst cover band. The track, along with other contributions such as favourite Christmas songs recorded by Bon Jovi, Madonna and Run DMC helped the project to raise over 8 million dollars from sales of 4 million plus albums worldwide for the Special Olympics International Ltd.

Then after collaborating with blues legend Woody Guthrie on the track *'Jesus Christ'* for the *'A Vision Shared'* benefit album in aid of The Smithsonian Institute in Washington, the group once again swept the board in The Rolling Stone magazine reader's poll. They walked away with Album of the year for *'The Joshua Tree'* and best single for *'With Or Without You'* among their eight awards that year.

That, however, paled into insignificance when compared with the honours bestowed upon the group at the 1988 Grammy Awards, the very pinnacle of achievements to be awarded by the music industry anywhere in the world.

The band members flew over to attend the awards ceremony held at New York's Radio City Music Hall and were honoured for their trouble by picking up the awards for Best Rock Performance by a group and Album of the year for *'The Joshua Tree'*. The recognition they had sought and craved for had been surpassed that evening.

# Chapter 13

## Inspirationally Speaking

U2 now began to spend time working on and building up to the release of a dual project *'Rattle And Hum'* the album and the movie.

The album attempted to couple alternative versions of live favourites, together with a number of new studio songs, with an interlinking theme of chronicling the band's influences, which of course were many and varied. The group conceded that *'Rattle And Hum's'* intention was to be an album made by Rock 'n' Roll fans, for their own.

During the previous American tour, on days off and during some predesignated dates the group had entered various studios including a stint at Memphis' Sun Studios, birthplace for the influential works of among others Elvis Presley and Carl Perkins.

The Sun Studios sound was a big influence on the group and during their time spent in the studios there they recorded some three tracks for inclusion on the *'Rattle And Hum'* album.

The success of *'The Joshua Tree'*, the enormity of which had surprised no one more than the group themselves, had placed them at a point in their careers where they seemed slightly unsure of which direction to take next. The album had indeed put them somewhat in 'icon' territory, with its sales and the Time, Newsweek and two Rolling Stone covers within the space of a year.

Suddenly they were a very attractive proposition to the mass produced blandness of 'Darren and Sharon' types, the sought of people who were readily buying the groups records, but who seemed unsure as to what had motivated them to do so in the first place.

In the aftermath of the release of *'Rattle And Hums'*, it was thought that the group had deliberately attempted to shake off around 50% of their audience, and although this was not necessarily achieved, a fair attempt was made at doing so.

*'Rattle And Hums'* criteria was to eliminate the familiar U2 'sound' and replace it for the albums purpose with a more erratic mixture of their influences, encompassing everything from the more straight forward rock approach to other fields of music such as Gospel, Country and Soul. The listeners to the album's finished results were not put off however, as Bono would later concede that *"as long as the songs are good, they'll go with us all the way"*.

*'Rattle And Hum'* was spread across a double album and single CD, and it was positively the most bizzare direction for the group to take at the time that they did. Just when everyone would have expected, anticipated and perhaps, (at least on the record companies side), wanted *'The Joshua Tree*, part two, they came up with what was a diverse, and at times far from easily digestible mixture of fresh new material and live versions of many older tracks.

The album, apart from being their most erratic and sprawling work to date, had the effect of spawning the seeds of what was to become the inevitable U2 backlash. This had been on the cards for some time, but the band had yet to slip up sufficiently enough to justify its wheels being set in motion. In many reviewers eyes though, the release of *'Rattle And Hum'* presented them with their long awaited opportunity to get the knives out for the group.

Reviews were quick to criticise the album's full throttle attempts to capture and categorise the diverse influences they had had, claiming that it resulted in a mish mash of sound. The combination of live tracks with new material was also criticised for giving the album no real sense of continuity or direction. Whereas the group had previously claimed to be without roots suddenly here they were with a whole new set of heroes and musical directions.

The album did, however, have its undisputed highlights. One of them being the collaboration with Harlem's New Voices Of Freedom gospel choir on a stirring interpretation of '*I Still Haven't Found What I'm Looking For*'. The idea for this came about when the choir recorded their own version of the song for release in America on a small independent record label in New Jersey. The choir's version had come to the attention of the group who were suitably impressed as to set up a meeting with its creators. At this meeting the idea of a collaboration between the group and the choir was soon discussed. This culminated with the New Voices Of Freedom choir joining the band onstage at New York's Madison Square Garden for a towering and majestic version of the song, subsequently captured on tape for use on the '*Rattle And Hum*' album.

The songs starts off with a semi acoustic delivery with minimal accompaniment, just Bono's and The New Voice's Choirs vocals for about two minutes, until it then takes off even further, hitting a new high with the full group's participation, before breaking loose again to its original semi acoustic feel, complimented this time by Adam's bass guitar. Stripped of its pop based origins, the song actually works remarkably easily and fully encapsulates and benefits from the new gospel treatment given to it in this new interpretation.

The rehearsals for this performance at the choirs Harlem church were also filmed for prosperity becoming one of '*Rattle And Hum*' the movie's undoubted highlights.

The only real draw back, not even really a criticism, is that to fully appreciate the inclusion and performance they gave of a track like '*I Still Haven't Found What I'm Looking For*', with The New Voices Of Freedom Choir, you really have to have been there or see some form of visual accompaniment, to fully appreciate it.

In keeping with the album's desire to pay homage to the group's favoured songs and artists, interpretations of songs from artists and groups as diverse as Jimi Hendrix, Bob Dylan and The Beatles were included.

A full throttle, hectic live version of The Beatles classic '*Helter Skelter*' was recorded during a performance at The Mc Nichols Arena in Denver, Colorado.

'*Helter Skelter*' opens the album, with Bono cryptically stating that Charles Manson had stolen the song from The Beatles, and that they were now stealing it back. What in reality he appeared to be hinting at, was that U2 were now in a position not a million miles away from the sort of giddy heights that The Beatles themselves had achieved some fifteen years earlier. All though that proclamation, of course, is open to debate. *'Helter Skelter'* is a very interesting choice of song to lead off the album however, and the group really attacks it head on, in a sort of style not so dissimilar to that of Siouxie And The Banshees version of a Beatles classic some years before, *'Dear Prudence'*. Although the choice of song was criticised somewhat in reviews, it has a definite quality in its ramshackle and 'throw everything at it and see what happens' approach.

The inclusion of this song is also a great success in my opinion, given that it was quite possibly the last sort of thing the audiences, (many of whom were no doubt seduced to go and see the band because of *'The Joshua Tree'*), were expecting to hear.

I remember a similar sort of occasion occurring at a live concert in 1983, when at the height of their popularity, as supposed teenybop icons, electro duo Soft Cell stunned their audience when returning for an encore by bursting into an hilariously inappropriate but totally triumphant version of the Suicide classic *'Ghostrider'*. This was much to the startled bemusement of the young girls, (and boys), at the front who were positively in a frenzy of excitement in anticipation of hearing *'Tainted Love'*, or such, as the encore. U2's version of *'Helter Skelter'*, evokes memories, and draws certain comparisons.

*'Van Diemen's Land'* follows *'Helter Skelter'*, another interesting departure for the group in that this song is both written and performed by The Edge. It's a semi acoustic Country and Western styled song, and the fact that the vocal is not for once delivered by Bono does make for a pleasing change for a U2 album. The only disappointment is that the song is faded out rather quickly just when it really starts to get going and become very interesting. It is however a track that works once again merely because it is not the sort of thing one would expect to hear on a U2 album especially around this time.

Another new track then appears, *'Hawkmoon 269'*, (the title of the song having been inspired by a road sign they saw whilst travelling in America, from the window of the tour bus). *'Hawkmoon 269'* was another of the tracks that marked a very different musical departure for the group. The track starts off with one of Larry's pounding drum patterns which then perfectly inter-twines with Bono's vocal and lyrics, in which he appears to be making declarations of unrequited love towards his chosen suitor. Bob Dylan pops up with some neat Hammond Organ work which nicely complements the general mood and up-lifting feel of the song. Backing vocalists take over the middle section of the song and help to draw it to a climatic, frenzied finale. It is by far one of the album's more experimentally veined highlights, and has enormous power and presence.

The somewhat bizzare mixture of the new tracks interspersed with live concert recordings then continues with a live version of Bob Dylan's *'All Along The Watchtower'* which the group had learnt , literally minutes before going on stage at a free concert in San Francisco, intriguingly named 'Save The Yuppie'. The song, that had originally been made famous by the late Jimi Hendrix, received a passionate vocal performance from Bono and inspired playing from the other band members, which made for yet another bizzare choice in material, but again one which worked surprisingly well.

The album's complete refusal to stay within any expected boundaries and conform, or stick with some sort of winning formula is illustrated by the inclusion of tracks such as *'Freedom For My People'*. Performed by two black street singers, it is a short inclusion on the album but one that makes you sit up when it comes on and take notice merely due to it being so unexpected.

*'Silver And Gold'*, the track originally written and performed solo by Bono for the Artist Against Apartheid album is given a live airing during the groups concert at the Mc Nichols Arena in Denver, and included on the *'Rattle And Hum'* album from that concert. It actually sounds far too crisp and clean though, (bar Bono's mid song explanation of the songs origin), to be a live version. Something which could not be said about the next track, a live version of *'Pride'*.

The album version of *'Pride'* was again recorded at the McNichols Arena in Denver, but the difference in crowd reaction between the two numbers is immense. With *'Pride'* the audience recognises the song from the moment the first note is played and duly scream their approval. They also take over the middle part of the song, particularly on the choruses, almost drowning out Bono's vocals. The only real criticism of the version of *'Pride'* that is included here is that it seems to be played at far too frantic a pace by the group. That aside, it is an obvious and enormous crowd pleaser and audience participation number and it is delivered by the group as such.

*'Angel Of Harlem'*, one of the new tracks written around this time and then included on the album is another number influenced by blues and swathed in an infectiously domineering horn sound. It was inspired by, and recorded as a tribute for the late Billie Holiday during the time the band spent in the Sun Studios complex in Nashville. This was later to become a Top ten single for the

group in the British charts, with the 12" and CD single versions of the song containing a live version of another of the albums tribute based tracks, 'Love Rescue Me'.

'Love Rescue Me' had been written with and originally dueted by Bono with Bob Dylan, a long time hero of the group's. (Although he mysteriously insisted that his lead vocal on the track was not used in the songs end result.). It's another of the album's slightly soulful sounding tracks, seemingly effortless, that dips into and makes a nod in the direction of these new found influences, without becoming too bogged down in painstakingly trying to reproduce them . It's one of those tracks that works well enough, but the curious vocal style adopted by Bono for the song does tend to grate somewhat after a while.

'Love Rescue Me' was one of the three songs recorded during the groups time in Sun Studios, along with the aforementioned 'Angel Of Harlem'. The other song recorded at Sun was 'When Love Comes To Town', to which blues legend B.B. King lent his considerable talents.

'When Love Comes To Town' is very much one of the album's best tracks. The song has an incredibly infectious up-tempo feel which carries it along effortlessly. One of Bono's more accomplished and confident sounding vocal performances, it works perfectly when combined with the throaty drawl of B.B. King. 'When Love Comes To Town' was also lifted for single release reaching Number 6 in the UK chart, the video of which featured rehearsals for the song, which were filmed in the studios at Sun in Memphis, and again produced what was certainly one of the more distinctive and memorable highlights of 'Rattle And Hum,' the film.

The released 'Rattle And Hum' had actually been preceded by the band's momentous achievement of attaining their first Number 1 single in the British charts.

Previously they had come agonisingly close with singles such as 'Pride' and 'With Or Without You', and while the albums had regularly hit the top of the charts, up till now that success with the singles had eluded them. 'Desire' provided the necessary breakthrough when it shot straight into the Top 40 of the British Singles chart at Number One, although it only managed to remain there for a solitary week, it had still been another achievement for the group.

The video of the song was a frantic succession of Americana influenced images, coupled with the songs up-beat Bo Didley sounding beat. As the bulk of the live sequences from 'Rattle And Hum' had been its performance parts were shot in stark black and white, which, mixed with the flashy colours and lights of the American travelogue style parts, made for an enthralling video.

The only other track to be released as a single in the UK didn't come out until June of 1989, when the album's delicate and beautiful closing track *'All I Want Is You'* was released reaching Number 4 in the British charts. The song was one that illustrated just how powerful and poignant the band could be without having to rely on the straight-in-your-face tactics of earlier years. The song actually evokes memories of the sort of peak they had hit on earlier songs such as *'Bad'*, which had certain similarities with *'All I Want Is You'*, particularly the song's guitar patterns. The single's success was no doubt helped by the fact that its video received a heavily trailed premiere in its own late night slot on British televisions Channel 4.

Elsewhere on the album there were tracks such as *'Heartland'*, which was pleasant enough but hardly set the album alight, and *'God Part II'*, dedicated to the memory of John Lennon. *'God Part II'*, another of the albums more up-tempo tracks, was one of those that gave a good indication of the direction the group would take, and develop further in subsequent years.

A distorted and muffled sounding taped version of Jimi Hendrix playing America's National Anthem *'The Star Spangled Banner'* is then played, serving as the fitting introduction for one of the groups most powerful songs when played live, *'Bullet The Blue Sky'*.

The version of *'Bullet The Blue Sky'* here was recorded in front of 60,000 fans at The Sun Devil Stadium in Temple, Arizona shortly before Christmas of 1987. As often happens when playing live versions of songs that were regular occurrences in the set-list, a certain degree of improvisation was introduced into the songs performance. This not only kept the songs fresh for the fans, many of whom would travel great distances to catch every show on the tour, but, also of course for the group themselves, meaning no degree of real complacency or monotony would set in. In this case that entailed Bono adding his own thoughts and impressions on the subject of TV evangelists, during the song's spoken closing section. During this he questions their general authenticity by first criticising them for procuring money from sick and defenseless people, and then adding, rather wittily, that to the best of his knowledge the God that he is aware of doesn't actually have a cash flow problem, and so why should people be sending their hard earned money to these 'TV preachers'. All in all a powerful and emotive penultimate track. The album then closes with the afore-mentioned *'All I Want Is You'*.

'*Rattle And Hum*' the film was given high profile premieres in two American cities, New York and Los Angeles as well as Madrid in Spain and inevitably Dublin.

The reviews for '*Rattle and Hum*', particularly from America, however were generally poor.

Most seized upon were the film's general lack of direction, the continuity problems created by having black and white footage one minute and colour the next and the actual purpose its existence served, other than highlighting what came across as self-congratulatory collaborations and performances. After the group's hard core of devoted fans had flocked to see it, general attendance began to dry up. This became most notably obvious in America where the U2 back lash it was fuelling began to affect record sales as well.

'*Angel Of Harlem*' had performed well enough in the Billboard charts, peaking at Number 14. But its follow up '*When Love Comes To Town*', could only manage a very disappointing Number 68. The problem further escalated when the final attempt at a big hit single from the album was thwarted. '*All I Want Is You*' endured an embarrassingly short life span on the chart spending a few short weeks there and peaking at Number 83.

In the meantime a major four months '*Love Town*' world tour was undertaken, significantly not visiting America, where the back lash bought on by '*Rattle And Hum*' had been most severe.

America it was decided could wait, and instead they toured on somewhat safer grounds in Europe, Australasia and their native Ireland, where the tour ended with four spectacular performances at The Point in Dublin. This included a concert broadcast live on New Year's Eve to millions of radio listeners throughout Europe.

Despite their undoubtedly huge and loyal following,( American fans had continued to show their support, voting them winners in eleven of the categories at that year's Rolling Stone readers' poll awards), '*Rattle And Hum*' had stagnated rather than developed and increased the band's popularity.

Although, as was previously stated, this may have well been intended, ultimately it was to prove frustrating and unsatisfying for the group. It seemed as if in order to progress as a band the time had come for a major upheaval and a general rethink of the band's motivations and of the direction they were taking.

The Dublin concerts at The Point were a fitting way for the group themselves to finish off a chapter of their history. It was where they had originated and grown to such extraodinary proportions, and from where they would now temporarily depart, taking a much needed break away from the media spotlight, spending time with family and friends, and be given the chance to reinvent and develop themselves. Something that they were to achieve with gusto.

# Chapter 14

## Invigoratingly Refreshed

'*The Joshua Tree*' had not only bought U2 fame but also most certainly fortune. It's success meant that the group were now financially secure for life and consequently were able to involve themselves in slightly more off the wall projects like '*Rattle And Hum*', artistic and financial gambles that were they to fail were not likely to destroy the band in the long term.

Many rumours about the possible demise of the band had began to circulate after Bono's on stage announcement during the last concert of the '*Love Town*' tour at The Point in Dublin that the band needed to "*go away for a while*". And although there was to be a two year absence until the next album, the band were anything but idle during that time.

Bono and The Edge provided the musical score for a Royal Shakespeare Companies production of Antony Burgess' 'A

Clockwork Orange', to varying degrees of critical acclaim. Some of the reviewers liked it, but the author himself, Anthony Burgess, was not impressed with their efforts calling it *"neo wallpaper"* and *"not music at all"*.

Larry Mullen helped to write and produced a single for the Republic Of Ireland's football team, intended to boost moral for their assault on the 1990 World Cup football tournament in Italy.

Also the somewhat inevitable 'guest' appearances were made, Bono joining Bob Dylan on stage as well as accompanying David Bowie for a number whilst he was undertaking his 1990 *Sound and Vision* world tour.

During 1990 the group were also paid tribute to when British soul group The Chimes covered *'I Still Haven't Found What I'm looking For'*, taking their version of the song, as U2 had before them, into the Top10 of the British singles chart.

A clue as to the intended direction the band were going to take with any new recordings was offered when the band contributed their highly original interpretation of the Cole Porter classic *'Night And Day'* to the *'Red Hot And Blue'* charity album. This was a charity release, the proceeds of which were to go towards funding the research into a cure for Aids.

Every song on the album featured a different group or artist giving their versions of Cole Porter classics. This resulted in many highlights such as Aztec Cameras cover of *"Do I Love You"*, Debbie Harry and Iggy Pop's rampant charge through *"Well Did You Evah"*, and indeed U2's *'Night And Day'*.

*'Night And Day'* was recorded in The Edge's basement during June of 1990. It was a distinctive musical departure for the group compared with their previous offerings, heavily employing the use of a smooth and yet sinister keyboard sound. Its somewhat European feel, coupled with its distinctive dance beat was a huge success, not just with the fans but also at club level, especially when given the remix treatment by acclaimed producer Youth.

Director Wim Wenders, noted for his work on *'An American Friend'* was approached and agreed to direct a video for the song, which was filmed at his house in Berlin and was included in a *'Red Hot And Blue'* television special.

Shortly after completing the filming for the video the group entered Berlin's Hansa 'by the wall' studios to begin work on the next album.

The studios had become a favoured haunt for many rock stars ever since being made famous by David Bowie after he recorded his *'Low'* and *'Heroes'* albums there. Subsequent users had included Iggy

Pop, Nick Cave and David Byrne, all, no doubt finding inspiration within Berlin's decaying decadence and splendour.

# Chapter 15

## New Dawnings

Original thoughts and ideas for the direction that the album would take were conceived as far back as September of 1989 when, during their Australian tour the group would pepper sound checks and on occasion live performances with snatches of ideas that would eventually form the basis of the new album's songs. Most of these impromptu spurts of melody ideas or riffs were recorded onto tape to be listened to later when a decision would be made as to whether or not they had any future potential.

Consequently, when the group entered the studio in Berlin they were armed with some thirty or so different tapes of ideas that had formulated themselves along the way.

These would be worked on and discussed whilst in the studio in Berlin, where the majority of the album patterns and ideas were conceived with the help of producer Daniel Lanois.

The time the group spent in Berlin became the subject of much interest when the master tapes of a rehearsal, and what was said to be a particularly lacklustre one at that, found their way out of the studio and inevitably onto the streets. They manifested themselves in the form of two poor quality bootleg albums *'Silver'* and *'Gold'* which found a ready and eager market in most places with copies being particularly prevalent in Germany, Holland and Britain.

When New Scotland Yard's Anti Fraud Squad became involved the distributors, whoever they were, obviously decided to lay low for a while and supplies dried up.

Those who did invest in a copy were probably very aggrieved to have parted with their money, as the albums contained little of interest to anyone, mainly consisting of just snatches of ideas and sounds that may or may not end up being used. How the tapes had come into existence in the first place still remains a mystery, although the inevitable conclusion was that someone, obviously an outsider, had taped one of the rehearsal sessions without the band's knowledge with the express interest in making a fast buck.

Just prior to the band relocating to Dublin to finish off work on the album, a cover version of *'Where The Streets Have No Name'* was incorporated into one of The Pet Shop Boys records.

A little bickering between the groups ensued when The Pet Shop Boys' Neil Tennant called Bono a hypocrite after Bono had heard the Pet Shop Boys' version of the song and had reportedly asked *"What have I, what have I, what have I done to deserve this?."*

In May of 1991, the U2 operation moved back to Ireland and into Elsinore near the sea at Dalkey that would be home for the next six months. Here the album would be finalised, chinks ironed out and final decisions made.

Elsinore, named after the Danish port in Shakespeare's Hamlet, is a huge refurbished mansion about ten miles from Dublin city. The house had been on the market seeking a selling price of around one million Irish punts, but when no immediate buyer was found it was negotiated for U2 to rent the house from its owner for the sum of 4,000 punts a week.

The house had been refurbished with chandeliers and huge fake fires leading Bono to comment that it was *"like something out of Twin Peaks."*

Two of the house's larger rooms were selected as being ideal for centering the recording process around and so steps were made to set them up for that purpose.

One of these rooms was a huge former ballroom with panoramic views of the ocean from its imposing bay windows, the other a slightly smaller room on the floor below where a more familiar studio style setting was created. The two rooms were both used for the recording process, occasionally simultaneously and were interlinked for continuity purposes by both microphones and video cameras.

The new material would be finished off here over the following months before being taken to the familiar setting of Windmill Studios in Dublin for the final mixing process.

During the forthcoming months, whilst work on the new album continued at Elsinore, the band member's lives all underwent changes in one form or another.

One of the sadder moments of this time was The Edge separating from wife Aislinn, and distress must also have been caused to Adam when Dublin County Council's road department approved a plan to build a motorway on the southern section of Dublin that would effectively pass right through his Rathfarnham estate.

Somewhat happier times though were the news that Bono's wife had given birth to their second child, named Eve, and that the Dublin Tourism Board were planning to erect two plaques in honour of the group, recognising their contribution to the Irish music industry.

# Chapter 16

## But What Does It Mean?

From the moment '*The Fly's*' opening guitar riff assaulted the airwaves in October of 1991, it was patently obvious that a new U2 had emerged during their self imposed two years exodus from the charts.

Whereas previous U2 singles had often gradually coaxed the listener in a soothing manner into gradually appreciating and absorbing the track at a safe distance, this one smacked you straight between the eyes.

After the polished smooth excesses of '*The Joshua Tree*' suddenly here was a harder edged, grittier sounding, guitar-riff orientated monster. The single had the air not particularly of an established band previewing a track from their seventh album, but of a new band's debut, fresh sounding and exciting.

The band's financial security had long since been guaranteed and it seemed artistic satisfaction was now the order of the day.

The single had what seemed to be a distinctly un-American feel, far more European influenced, no doubt bought on by the time spent in Berlin.

'The Fly' shot straight to the top of the British singles chart to give the group their second Number 1 single in Britain.

A heavily criticised marketing ploy was initiated for 'The Fly's' release whereby it would only be available in the shops for three weeks, then deleted.

Whether or not this tactic was instrumental towards its attaining the Number 1 position in the singles chart is of course debatable.

Even though it was only available for three weeks it was still possible to buy it for a short period after and inevitably it also soon became available as an import single as well.

When the video was shown on the following week's Top Of The Pops it became apparent that the group had undergone not just a musical change, but a distinct visual one as well. The group all looked assuredly confident, without necessarily attaining an air of cockiness, shades, bandannas and slick-backed hair were the dominant images portrayed by the group members.

A first clue was also offered by 'The Fly's' video as to the direction that the groups future live 'Zoo TV' concerts would take.

Slogans that would become readily familiar over the next few months such as "Watch More TV", "Everything you know is wrong" were flashed across the TV screens that adorned the video background, in quick succession .

Prior to the album's release in November the band had maintained an effective media silence, when they did give interviews they were selective in the extreme.

In one of the granted interviews to Musician magazine, The Edge explained how part of the thinking behind 'Achtung Baby', from the band's point of view, was an attempt to distance themselves from what was effectively the 'U2 myth'.

This meant not assaulting the market straight out with an obvious single, but confusing them somewhat by releasing what was effectively an experimental type single for the group with 'The Fly'.

This, along with the effective media silence meant that when 'Achtung Baby' was released in November nobody knew quite what to expect.

Whether the media and critics knew what to expect or not soon became irrelevant, as when 'Achtung Baby's' reviews arrived they were generally very good.

The first image and indeed departure for the group from previous incarnations was apparent from the sleeve of the album itself.

Whereas previous album covers for the group had consisted of singular or soft focus photographs, here suddenly there was a virtual riot of images and visuals on display. The front cover itself sported some sixteen different snap-shot type photos encompassing everything from the East German Trabant car ( now readily associated with U2), a star of sequins, two separate cheap looking silver rings bearing the letters U and 2 and Bono in what looks like heavily made up black mascaraed eyes, posing with a topless model. Once inside, the music itself was just as suprising.

The album's opening track 'Zoo Station' at first seemed far too hectic and confused sounding, as if three different songs were trying to merge themselves into one. Select magazine implied that the track was in fact a complete shambles, but with subsequent listenings its at first disjointed feel jelled together to form a stark, effective opening track.

'Zoo Station's' strength was in its approach. Whereas on previous albums songs would often come across as grossly over structured and formulated, here everything was thrown together in an almost ramshackle approach and yet it was ultimately still digestible.

'Zoo Stations' frank approach, also apparent on 'The Fly' single, was used again on 'Until The End Of The World', (written for inclusion in Wim Wenders film of the same name along with tracks by the likes of REM) which was structured around a shuffling guitar riff resplendently complementing the sheer stubborn approach of the drum patterns.

The group's breast-beating histrionics of yore suddenly seemed a million miles away from this fresh, urgent sounding new material.

The album's lyrical preoccupations seemed concerned with relationships and strife. And along with Bono's at times angst ridden vocals, these themes dominated the majority of the tracks. None perhaps more effectively as on one of the album's slower tracks the tender, poignant sounding 'Trying To throw Your Arms Around The World', which had an almost dream-like, ethereal quality.

This theme was also apparent on 'So Cruel', Bono's tortured vocal perfectly complementing the track's dark piano hook and effective use of a string arrangement, spotlighting on the violin and viola.

Perhaps the album's most commercially appealing song on first listen and what was indeed to become the second single release from the album was *'Mysterious Ways'*.

The single seemed to be taking a nod in the direction of, and acknowledging the success of the band at the time who were gathering huge record sales and becoming the ultimate press darlings, like The Happy Mondays and The Charlatans, but at the same time it effectively out-bagged these baggies, as they were known, with its confident swagger and irresistible dance feel. There were no Hammond organs or spaced out dancers in sight, but it was still a fresh and invigorating sound. Somewhat surprisingly the single only reached Number 13 in the British singles chart, although it did give them a Top 10 single in the Billboard singles chart in America, particularly satisfying as *'The Fly'* had not really taken off there at all.

The single's release in Britain made no secret of its dance orientated aspirations with the CD single and 12" versions carrying four different mixes of just the one song.

This new found 'dance' element to their music was further explored by the release of *'Even Better Than The Real Thing'.*

Soon after the singles original format version had dropped out of the chart, it was replaced by a whole new set of remixes by such respected individuals in that field as Paul Oakenfold, Steve Osborne and Apollo 440. These new mixes christened with such names as *"The Perfecto Mix"* and *"Sexy Dub Mix"* were to prove immense floor fillers in the clubs and confirmed the band's new found status, (with a little help from the remixer's), in that area. That, together with the video for the song, (acclaimed for the revolutionary techniques used in the camera work), helped to make *'Even Better Than The Real Thing'* one of the album's more wholly satisfying ventures.

*'Ultra Violet'* (Light My Way) sounded somewhat unpromising at first. Its opening couple of semi-spoken, semi-sung lines coming across like a pseudo Simple Minds, but it built into yet another heavily guitar orientated work out to great effect.

*'Acrobat'* on the other hand suffered in that it was a little bit too muddled and jumbled in places. Whereas *'The Fly'* or *'Zoo Station'* had used this chaotic method of assembling a song to great effect, *'Acrobat'* tried but failed, principally because it was unable to retain enough of the seemingly effortless melodies that were created to such great effect elsewhere. Also Bono's vocal delivery of the song appeared just a little too forcibly angst ridden and taut as to suggest complete authenticity.

The album's closing track *'Love Is Blindness'* suffered from pretty much the same problems as *'Acrobat'* and so it was somewhat suprising to learn that whereas *'Acrobat'* was not, initially at least, used in the live shows, *'Love Is Blindness'* was featured as one of the encores.

The albums two other tracks *'One'* and *'Who's Gonna Ride Your Wild Horses'*, were both very much more recognizably created by U2, neither would have fitted in with the context of say *'The Joshua Tree'*, but there were certain elements that made them unmistakably familiar.

Both, ironically became future single releases. *'Who's Gonna Ride Your Wild Horses'* carried on in the wake of *'Mysterious Ways'* and *'Even Better Than The Real Thing'* and was released in a radically different form to the album version having a far more dance orientated feel to it.

And *'One'*, a softer, more delicate song more in the vein of *'Trying To Throw Your Arms Around The World'* or *'So Cruel'* was most notable upon its release for the news that all proceeds from its sales would be going to a nominated Aids charity. Although, in a later Radio interview when asked if there was any particular reason that the group had chosen this song in order to make this gesture, there was noticeable reluctance on the part of Adam, who answered the question, to explain why this song was chosen.

The album debuted at Number 1 in both Britain and America, although it had a fight on its hands to retain that position in the States, facing as it did tough competition for the top slot from the likes of the new Michael Jackson album and the huge selling Country and Western star Garth Brooks. Although its first week sales there of well over a quarter of a million copies were impressive enough in itself.

Its general critical success and the subsequent exposure bought on by the *'Zoo TV'* live dates have seen it spend well over a year so far in the British charts and with the live summer dates coming up that situation seems unlikely to change.

Some three months after the album's release the group broke their long maintained media silence in Britain when they gave an exclusive and unexpected live interview to Radio 1's Mark Goodier evening show.

The interview caught the band in a relaxed and somewhat jovial mood, however the whole of the interview had an air of nervousness on the part of its host, obviously due to the fact that it was being broadcast live, with no possibility existing of going back later to edit out any embarrassment that may or may not occur during the transmission.

Mark Goodier started by asking why the band had maintained this silence and supposed reluctance to talk to the media in general about the album. The band's response was that they were tired of the treadmill they had to undergo whenever a new album was completed and subsequently released. Immediately having to jump aboard some promotional train and endure an endless succession of largely meaningless and unfullfilling interviews. Merely being asked the same questions, to which there could only be the same answers, over and over again.

The Edge was asked about this new found dance element within their music, and basically whether or not they were merely jumping on board with the latest trend, by pursuing their new found interest in it.

His particularly inspired reply was to state that he thought that they had always been a dance act, but it was only when he had tried to dance to one of the songs, that he discovered that in fact they were not.

On the subject of the heavily bootlegged tapes from the sessions recorded in Berlin, Bono commented that, *"people are charging a lot of money for something that is not very good, it was like having your notebook read out. That's the bit I didn't like about it. There were no great undiscovered works, (on the tapes), it was just gobbledygook."*

The interview threw up many humorous moments, such as when asked to comment on the rumours that were circulating in the music press at the time, that the support group for British concerts would be Carter The Unstoppable Sex Machine that *"we won't have people in short trousers on our tour"*, (a reference to Carter's favoured attire at the time).

There was also a rather bizzare conversation during the interview when the subject of the merits of an organisation like the BBC was put up against the commercial radio stations. Bono had his own argument for pledging his support to the commercial free stations, and this was brought to light when he and The Edge started discussing a programme Bono had (allegedly) heard on the BBC World Service the previous week.

The conversation went something like this. Bono, *"I love the BBC. On the world service last week I was listening to an hour-long programme on owl droppings."* The Edge, *"Owl droppings? hold on a second! Owl droppings?"* Bono again, *'Yes, it was an on the spot report, on the tawny owl. I kid you not, it was brilliant."* Edge, *"So what was the story on owl droppings?"* Bono *"The furry vole...that seemed to be his major diet. They were going through the whole thing. It was brilliant.*

*Now you would never get that on a commercial station, let's be honest."*

The interview progressed for a while in this light hearted manner taking in the reasons for the group's refusal to accept corporate sponsorship, their failure to deliver a half-promised Radio 1 session, (the reason given by Adam was that it was practically impossible to get them all in the same room at the same time these days), and the reason the interview was being filmed by the band's own camera crew, which according to The Edge was because they were all too busy to write diaries for themselves these days and so they had a camera crew follow them around to record what happens to them, where they've been and what they've done so they can look back at it later. *"Planet Narcissus"* as Bono put it.

Another conversation followed on the debate about the criticism that having '*The Fly*' single on general release for just three weeks had caused. The band's justifiable explanation on the merits of this, (although it had actually been the record company's idea), was that it meant that because it was the new U2 single, radio stations both here and in America would play it, despite its somewhat uncommercial feel, and that, they as a group were in a position to abuse the power they had, and they intended to have a good time doing precisely that.

The last word in the interview typically went to Bono when, after Mark Goodier's statement that, *"we'll have to leave it there because there's somebody more important than you coming up on the radio"*. Bono's droll reply was *"Mark, I doubt it"*.

# Chapter 17

## Slow Cars And Bright Stars

Bono's parting comment to Radio 1's Mark Goodier on finishing their interview was one that was certainly echoed by the majority of the crowd in the Lakeland Arena, Florida, for the first night of the 'Zoo TV' tour.

The 6,000 tickets available for the concert, that had reportedly sold out in around four minutes, and the fever pitch of the eagerly anticipatory crowd in the arena was testament enough to the demand to witness the first American concerts by U2 in some four years plus.

The welcome they were afforded upon their return to American shores was not far from being one that jubilant troops might anticipate upon returning from a glorious victory, or that a newly elected president could expect when returning to a faithful constituency.

The reception that had started in Florida was set to stay with them all the way through the American tours thirty-two arena dates that would finish for the time being in Vancouver, Canada near the end of April and return to tackle the much larger stadiums, from where they had departed America in 1987, once again in the summer.

'Zoo TV' was a live visual extravaganza, the likes of which had previously been attempted (most notably by The Pet Shop Boys), but which until now had not been pulled off to such great effect.

The most notably visual aspect of the stage set itself was undoubtedly the six East German Trabant cars suspended above the stage which were painted in various bright colours and adorned with either flower designs or daubed with slogans. The cars' headlights had been removed to be replaced with strong spot-lights that would track the band members movements around the stage.

There were also four large video screens and around twenty smaller sized TV 's that would flash up various phrases or words throughout the band's performance. These would consist of slogans such as "Its Your World You Can Change It", "Cry More Often", "Call Your Mother", "Remember What You Dream" and "Everything You Know Is Wrong", as well as buzz-words like "Psycho", "Sex", "Drugs", "Death", "Napalm", and "Paranoia" all flashed across the screens in quick succession.

These screens would remain active long after the words and slogans had finished, cameras would track the audience activity , as well as what was happening on stage and relay it onto the giant screens. Plus they would pick up various cable television shows and transmit whatever was being broadcast at the time. Also, key images or footage would be used to enhance a particular song they were playing, a picture of Martin Luther King during *'Pride'* for example, or fires burning within cross shaped frames for *'Bullet The Blue Sky'*.

Another inventive departure, not usual for a rock-orientated show, was the employing of a belly dancer, Christina Petro. The story goes that she had contacted the band to ask if they needed the services of a belly dancer, was given an audition, subsequently hired and soon became a part of the tour. Her big moment being to shimmy on stage during *'Mysterious Ways'*, and so give the song a bit more than just its dance appeal.

Undoubtedly one of the highlights of the show, not just for the fans, but for the group, and particularly Bono, would be when a telephone would appear on stage and he would make a call.

This would invariably be to The White House in Washington,

where he would request a couple of words with the (then) President of The United States, or *"Is George in?"*, as he would put it.

On another occasion the phone was used to place an order on a home shopping network, (which was showing on the video screens at the time), where he purchased an electric toaster.

And another time, when during a concert in Detroit an advertisement for a local pizza parlour came on to a live transmission that the video screens had picked up, to which Bono's response was to ring up and order ten thousand pizzas for the crowd. Evidently the pizza parlour took the order but given the time limitations was only able to come up with around one thousand pizzas which were duly delivered to the arena and handed out to be devoured by the first few rows of the audience.

At the front of all this was the band, led by Bono dressed in black leather and wrap around shades, portraying a fictional egomaniac character named *'The Fly'*. As the tour progresses many other names or persona would be christened for him or on his behalf, everything from 'The New Lizard King' to a living reincarnation of Soft Cell's 'Sex Dwarf'. For the encores Bono reappeared in a Elvis style gold lame suit, that wouldn't have looked out of place in a Las Vegas revue. A mirror had been placed centre stage which he would turn to at one point and mockingly tell himself how wonderful he was. An egomaniac with a sense of humour.

The set list for the shows obviously drew heavily from the *'Achtung Baby'* material, opening each night as on the album with a faithful rendition of *'Zoo Station'*.

Two songs from *'Rattle and Hum'* were included, *'Angel Of Harlem'*, played acoustically mid-set, and *'Desire'*, the first of the encores.

Also the stronger, more stadium orientated material from *'The Joshua Tree'* (*'Bullet The Blue Sky'*, *'With or Without You'*, *'Where The Streets Have No Name'*, etc...), as well as the perennial live favourites *'Bad'* and *'Pride'* (In The Name Of Love).

One of the tour's undoubted highlights was once again when the group arrived in New York to play at the prestigious surroundings of Madison Square Garden in late March of 1992.

It was the group's first live concert in the city for five years and the hype and build up to their arrival was testament to the fact that they were welcomed back.

For weeks on end, local radio stations there had been running contests to win tickets which had become like gold dust since the dates they had sold out in under half an hour.

Those unfortunate enough not to have bought tickets in

advance, or won one of the many radio station contests, had to barter with the many and numerous tickets touts outside the venue, who were charging anything upwards of two hundred dollars for a single ticket.

The story was pretty much the same for the group throughout this arena based tour. It became patently obvious that in order to satisfy the huge demand for tickets when they returned to play America again, it would be for outdoor and stadium sized shows, as had been the case when they last played there.

This also proved to be the case in Britain, where, after playing at the 18,000 capacity Earls Court in June of '92, their next visit, which would be during the summer a year later, saw the band booked to play in the somewhat more spacious surroundings of the 80,000 capacity Wembley Stadium, for two nights.

As the tour progressed through 1992, many memorable and interesting moments were to occur.

The band told the story to Q magazine about their meeting with the then hopeful presidential candidate Bill Clinton.

Bono, *"We were in Chicago, and he was staying in the same hotel. We tried to wake him up (by phone) at three o'clock in the morning for one of those late night chats"*.

Edge, *"There were a few bevies involved, I have to say. Somebody stumbled off to knock on Bill's door, only to run into four dozen Secret Service guys in the corridor. We realised then that it was even harder to meet him than it is to meet one of us."*

Bono, *"But they did pass on the message, and Bill came knocking on the door next day, which was very cool of him, and we shot the shit with the now president."*

Suddenly it would seem that if they were to continue with the onstage prank of phoning up the White House live for a chat with the President, now, they might actually get through and succeed in doing just that.

As *'Zoo TV's* live concert dates continue throughout what is likely to be the majority of 1993, moving from the smaller arenas into the giant football stadiums, the group have had time to reflect on its success and what it has meant to them individually.

One of the most intriguing aspects about *'Zoo TV '*has been the character that Bono portrays whilst on stage, *'The Fly'*. Where did it come from? Where is it going? And what makes it tick? In an interview with Rolling Stone magazine's Alan Light in Dublin, he tried answering a few of these questions.

He had among other things , this to say, *"I don't know, I've said it before, but there were reports of egomania, and I just decided to become everything they said I was. I felt like I didn't recognise the person I was meant to be as far as what you saw in the media. There's some kind of rape that happens when you are in the spotlight, and you go along with it."* Asked if he thought that turning up for events such as the demonstration at Sellafield against the nuclear processing plant in *'The Fly'* character, was damaging he said.*"Well I always thought of "The Fly' as a melt down kind of guy. I don't want to put too much emphasis on this character, but you gotta find new ways to say the same thing. I don't think its a contradiction to find yourself on the beach at a nuclear power plant wearing those sunglasses. I think its very surreal, and it was amusing to us even then. We were aware of how ridiculous it was ."*

He also spoke of how his relationship with his father had progressed and improved over the years. How he had been unsure of what reactions to expect from him and how he was surprised when he received compliments from him. He was then asked the age old question about whether or not he thought his father actually liked and enjoyed the music, to which he replied, *"I think he likes the music now, he'll say I like this one or I don't like that one, he's full of opinions. I'm really enjoying my father at the moment, I put him in the "One' video'.*

Asked about *'Achtung Baby'*, and what had inspired and driven them to achieve what they did with it, he said, *"One word, rhythm. Which is the sex of music. That was the thing we needed I think. It's a different place that was necessary for us to go to in the light of the new subject matter. You can't write songs about sex if you don't have it in the music."* This subject of sex and its many manifestations arising on *'Achtung Baby'* was further explored. Bono, *"I'd often found the sort of neon light aspects of sex very funny, the leather and lace aspect. It wasn't a sexuality that I particularly related to but its the one on every street corner, and so I got into it, and its great! Its just something I'm trying to understand, and I understand it a lot better having dressed up as a con man for the last year"*

He was finally asked if he had any intention of and how he was going to dispense with *'The Fly'* image, and if it had in fact taken over his life, to which he replied. *"We're in the middle of it right now (with Zoo TV), but the music tells you what to do. The music tells you what clothes to wear, what stage to stand on, who should photograph you, etc. Oscar Wilde said something like "The mask tells you more about the man". But its the music that tells you what to do. And if I want to take the glasses off (and lose the character), I just gotta change my tune."*

And so the band rolls on, many rumours will circulate as to what they are going to do next, but for the immediate future the band seem to be continuing the *'Zoo TV'* Tour. This was to have included a massive free concert in Dublin, which disappointingly had to be dropped due to the enormous financial costs involved in staging it. There were also worries about the safety aspects of holding such an event, especially in the after math of such tragedies as, for example what happened at Hillsborough. In stead of the one free concert the group decided to stage three extra Irish dates to which the previously unprecedented move was made of seeking and accepting some form of corporate sponsorship to help stage them. This was not for the obvious, or usual, reasons however, as it was soon revealed that any money raised from this sponsorship, (estimated at anything up to half a million pounds), would be evenly distributed among a number of Dublin based charities.

It would appear that a new studio based U2 album could be some time off yet, but plans are afoot for new recordings to be unleashed on an eager public sometime during the summer of 1993, when an EP of four songs is expected to be released.

What shape or form these new recordings will take remains a mystery, although it is rumoured that the band have been meeting and possibly recording with Johnny Cash and Bob Dylan, so that could be a clue as to the eventual out come.

As for now, the story continues...

Chapter 18

## Getting The Message Across
## (U2's involvement with Greenpeace).

During 1992 the group became heavily involved with many issues close to their hearts .

Long time members of the environmental protection group Greenpeace, they played at a benefit for the organisation in Manchester and attended a demo by Greenpeace about the plans to expand the processing capacity at The British National Fuels Sellafield plant.

The benefit concert at the 10,000 capacity G-Mex, saw U2 top a bill which also consisted of Public Enemy, Kraftwerk and Bad II.

Their highly entertaining set was topped off by being joined on stage by Lou Reed for a duet of his song *Satellite Of Love*.

The performance also contained the inevitable phone call which this time was to The Prime Minister's residence in Downing Street, London, where Bono was unable to obtain a few words with the Prime Minister, but told the somewhat bemused secretary to give him a message, along the lines that he should watch more TV.

After the concert, whilst various minor celebrities were taking full advantage of the hospitality on offer, the band took to a boat as part of a protest, which was of course the reason why they were there.

Bono speaking on why the band were taking part in this protest stated that the Irish shoreline, which is actually closer to Sellafield than to Downing Street London, (hence the telephone call during the concert), was already being affected by Sellafield's radioactive emissions.

The BNFL had attempted to gain a high court injunction preventing any protests taking place on their land, but this problem was got around by the protesters, and the group, taking to boats in the water in order to air their protests.

Once back ashore the demo continued, outside the lines which marked the end of the BNFL's land, with the group, all wearing protective clothing, depositing a number of barrels which contained contaminated mud from the Irish sea, (caused by Sellafield).

The involvement with Greenpeace, still continuing today, took a further step forward in the plans to try and prevent the opening of Sellafield 2 when other celebrities became involved as well, these included Vanessa Redgrave, Sting, Peter Gabriel, Michael Hutchence of INXS and Annie Lennox who all pledged support, which had the effect of encouraging some 40,000 members of the public to write letters of protest to Her Majesty's Inspectorate Of Pollution.

The effect of this letter writing strategy was that, because of the sheer numbers of protesters involved it would mean that the governing body, the Inspectorate Of Pollution, would be forced into holding a public inquiry about the Sellafield proposal.

The protesters main focus of argument against the proposed Sellafield 2 was that it was not just a national issue but that if it was allowed to continue it could easily become an international one. There was also the extraordinary costs involved.

Many of these issues were brought up by U2 in a letter to the British Government.

They brought to light the fact that over two billion pounds of British tax payers money had already been spent on Sellafield 2 and that it would cost at least another billion to see the proposed project through.

The potential for enormous environmental disasters were well catalogued, along with the possible outcome that many people could be affected by radioactive discharges. These issues and many more were also bought up in letters from some of the other protesters. However, up to this point the problems remain unsolved.

## SINGLES

(All singles listed below are done so in their original versions at the time of release, subsequent reissues on CD single, etc, are not always taken into consideration for these purposes) .

**Title:** *U23*
**Format:** 7"
**Main Track:** *Out Of Control.*
**Other Tracks:** *Stories For Boys/Boy-Girl.*
**Catalogue Number:** CBS 7951
**Produced by:** Chas De Whalley/U2
*Release Date:* September 1979.
*Additional Information:* This was the group's first recording , a three track EP only available in their native Ireland.

**Title:** *Another Day*
**Format:** 7"
**Other Track:** *Twilight.*
**Catalogue Number:** CBS 8306
**Produced By:** Chas De Whalley.
**Release Date:** February 1980.
**Additional Information:** This release was also made available only in Ireland.

**Title:** *11 O'Clock, Tick, Tock*
**Format:** 7"
**Other Track:** *Touch.*
**Catalogue Number:** Island WIP 6601
**Produced By:** Martin Hamnett.
**Release Date:** May 1980.
**Additional Information:** The group's first release for Island Records, and their first British Single.
**Chart Position:** (No Entry).

**Title:** *A Day Without Me*
**Format:** 7"
**Other Track:** *Things To Make And Do.*
**Catalogue Number:** WIP 6601
**Produced By:** Steve Lillywhite
**Release Date:** August 1980
**Additional Information:** The group's first work with producer Steve LillyWhite, who would go on to produce their first three albums.
**Chart Position:** (No Entry).


**Title:** *I Will Follow*
**Format:** 7"
**Other Track:** *Boy-Girl.*
**Catalogue Number:** WIP 6656
**Produced by:** Steve Lillywhite.
**Release Date:** October 1980.
**Additional Information:** *Boy-Girl* was a rerecorded version of the song which appeared on their first EP, U23.
**Chart Position:** (No Entry).


**Title:** *Fire*
**Format:** 7"/ 7" Double pack/ 12"
**Other Tracks:**
**7";** *J. Swallow.*
**7" Double Pack;** *Cry/The Electric Co./11 O'Clock, Tick, Tock./The Ocean (live version).*
**12";** *11 O'Clock, Tick, Tock./The Ocean (Live Version).*
**Catalogue Number:** WIP 6679
**Produced By:** Steve Lillywhite.
**Release Date:** June, 1981.
**Highest Chart Position:** Number 35
**Weeks On Chart:** 6

**Title:** *Gloria*
**Format:** 7".
**Other Track:** *I Will Follow (Live version)*
**Catalogue Number:** WIP 6733
**Produced By:** Steve Lillywhite.
**Release Date:** October, 1981.
**Highest Chart Position:** Number 55
**Weeks On Chart:** 4


**Title:** *A Celebration*
**Format:** 7"
**Other Tracks:** *Trash/Trampoline And The Party Girl.*
**Catalogue Number:** WIP 6770
**Produced By:** Steve Lillywhite.
**Release Date:** October, 1982.
**Highest Chart Position:** Number 47
**Weeks On Chart:** 4
**Additional Information:** Not available on any U2 albums.


**Title:** *New Year's Day*
**Format:** 7" and 7" Double Pack.
**Other Tracks:**
**7";** *Treasure.*
**7" Double Pack;** *Fire/I Threw A Brick Through A Window/A Day Without Me* (Live Version).
**Catalogue Number:** WIP 6848.
**Produced By:** Steve Lillywhite.
**Release Date:** January, 1983.
**Highest Chart Position:** Number 10
**Weeks On Chart:** 8


**Title:** *Two Hearts Beat As One*
**Format:** 7"/12' and Double Pack versions.
**Other Tracks:**
**7":** *Endless Deep.*
**12"** and Double Pack versions: *New Years Day/Two Hearts Beat As One* (American Remix).

**Catalogue Number:** IS 109.
**Produced By:** Steve Lillywhite.
**Release Date:** March, 1983.
**Highest Chart Position:** Number 18
**Weeks On Chart:** 5

**Title:** *Pride (In The Name Of Love)*
**Format:** 7" and 12".
**Other Tracks:**
**7":** *Boomerang.*
**12":** *Boomerang II/4th Of July.*
**Catalogue Number:** IS 202.
**Produced By:** Brian Eno/Daniel Lannois.
**Release Date:** September, 1984.
**Highest Chart Position:** Number 3.
**Weeks On Chart:** 11
**Additional Information:** The group's first release with the then new and experimental production team of Brian Eno and Daniel Lannois.

**Title:** *The Unforgettable Fire.*
**Format:** 7"/7" Double Pack/12'.
**Other Tracks:**
**7":** *A Sort Of Homecoming* (Live version).
**7" Double pack:** *Love Comes Tumbling/Thirty Seconds In Kingdom Come.*
**12":** *Love Comes Tumbling/The Three Sunrises.*
**Catalogue Number:** IS 220
**Produced By:** Brian Eno/ Daniel Lannois/Tony Visconti.
**Release Date:** April, 1985.
**Highest Chart Position:** Number 6.
**Weeks On Chart:** 6

**Title:** *With Or Without You.*
**Format:** 7"
**Other Tracks:** *Luminous Times (Hold On To Love)/Walk To The Water.*

**Catalogue Number:** IS 319.
**Produced By:** Daniel Lannois/Brian Eno.
**Release Date:** March, 1987.
**HIghest Chart Position:** Number 4
**Weeks On Chart:** 11
**Additional Information:** *'With Or Without You'* was mixed by Steve Lillywhite. It was also the group's first American Number 1 single.

**Title;** *I Still Haven't Found What I'm Looking For.*
**Format;** 7".
**Other Tracks;** *Spanish Eyes/Deep In The Heart.*
**Catalogue Number;** IS 340.
**Produced By;** Daniel Lannois/Brian Eno.
**Release Date;** May, 1987.
**Highest Chart Position;** Number 6
**Weeks On Chart;** 11

**Title;** *Where The Streets Have No Name.*
**Format;** 7'/12"/Cassette.
**Other Tracks;**
**7";** *Silver And Gold/Sweetest Thing.*
**12";** *Silver And Gold/Sweetest Thing/Race Against Time.*
**Cassette;** *Silver And Gold/Sweetest Thing/Race Against Time.*
**Catalogue Number;** IS 340.
**Produced By;** Daniel Lannois/Brian Eno.
**Release Date;** August, 1987.
**Highest Chart Position;** Number 4
**Weeks On Chart;** 6
**Additional Information;** *'Where The Streets Have No Name'* became U2's third consecutive American Number 1 single following *'With Or Without You'* and *'I Still Haven't Found What I'm Looking For'*.

**Title;** *In God's Country.*
**Format;** 7".
**Other Tracks;** *Bullet The Blue Sky/Running To Stand Still.*

**Catalogue Number;** (Island US Single). 7-99385.
**Produced By;** Daniel Lannois/Brian Eno.
**Release Date;** November, 1987.
**Highest Chart Position;** Number 48.
**Weeks On Chart;** 4
**Additional Information;** *In God's Country'* was a single only intended for release onto the American market. However the huge number of import copies that flooded into Britain and the subsequent sales, resulted in the single entering the lower regions of the British Singles Chart.

**Title;** *Desire.*
**Format;** 7' and 12".
**Other Tracks;**
**7";** *Hallelujah (Here She Comes)*
**12";** *Desire* (Hollywood Mix).
**Catalogue Number;** IS 400
**Produced By;** Jimmy Lovine.
**Release Date;** September, 1988.
**Highest Chart Position;** Number 1
**Weeks At Number 1;** 1.
**Weeks On Chart;** 8
**Additional Information;** U2's first British Number 1 Single.

**Title;** *Angel Of Harlem.*
**Format;** 7"/12"/CD single.
**Other Tracks;**
**7";** *A Room At The Heartbreak Hotel*
**12";** *Love Rescue Me* (Live version)
**CD single;** *Love Rescue Me* (Live version).
**Catalogue Number;** IS 402
**Produced By;** Jimmy Lovine.
**Release Date;** December, 1988.
**Highest Chart Position;** Number 9
**Weeks On Chart;** 6
**Additional Information;** The live version of *'Love Rescue Me'* on the 12" and CD single versions feature contributions with Keith Richards and Ziggy Marley And The Melody Makers.

**Title;** *When Love Comes To Town*
**Format;** 7' and 12'
**Other Tracks;**
**7";** *Dancing Barefoot*
**12";** *When Love Comes To Town (Live From The Kingdom Mix)/God Part II (Hard Metal Dance Mix).*
**Catalogue Number;** IS 411
**Produced By;** Jimmy Lovine
**Release Date;** April, 1989.
**Highest Chart Position;** Number 6.
**Weeks On Chart;** 7
**Additional Information;** The *'When Love Comes To Town' (Live From The Kingdom Mix)*, features the group in collaboration with Little Richard.

**Title;** *All I Want Is You*
**Format;** 7"/12" and CD Single.
**Other Tracks;**
**7";** *Unchained Melody.*
**12";** *Unchained Melody/Everlasting Love*
**CD Single;** (As above).
**Catalogue Number;** IS 422.
**Produced By;** Jimmy Lovine.
**Release Date;** June, 1989.
**Highest Chart Position;** Number 4.
**Weeks On Chart;** 6

**Title;** *Night And Day*
**Format;** 12"
**Tracks;** *Night And Day (Twilight Remix)/Night And Day (Steel String Mix)*
**Catalogue Number;** RHB 1
**Produced By;** The Edge/Paul Barrett.
**Remixed By;** Youth.
**Release Date;** December, 1990.
**Additional Information;** This was a limited edition 12" only promo issue single to raise money to benefit Aids research. It features remixed versions of the Cole Porter song that the group contributed to the *'Red, Hot Blue'* charity album.

**Title;** *The Fly*
**Format;** 7"/12" and CD Single.
**Other Tracks;**
**7";** *Alex Descends Into Hell For A Bottle Of Milk: Korova 1.*
**12";** *(As Above)/The Lounge Fly Mix.*
**CD Single;** (Same as 12").
**Catalogue Number;** IS 500.
**Produced By;** Daniel Lannois.
**Release Date;** October, 1991.
**Highest Chart Position;** Number 1.
**Weeks On Chart;** 9
**Additional Information;** *'The Fly'* was only on general and official release in Britain for three weeks. (Although it was still possible to obtain import versions of the single long after this time).

**Title;** *Mysterious Ways*
**Format;** 7"/12" and CD Single.
**Other Tracks;**
**7";** *Mysterious Ways (Solar Plexus Magic Hour Remix).*
**12";** *Mysterious Ways (Solar Plexus Extended Club Mix)/(Apollo 440 Magic Hour Remix)/(Tabla Motown Remix)/Solar Plexus Club Mix).*
**CD Single;** (As above).
**Catalogue Number;** IS 509.
**Produced By;** Daniel Lannois/Brian Eno.
**Release Date;** December, 1991.
**Highest Chart Position;** Number 13.

**Title;** *One*
**Format;** 7"/12" and CD Single
**Other Tracks;**
**7";** *'Satellite Of Love'*
**12";** *'Night And Day' (Steel String Remix)*
**CD Single;** (As above).
**Catalogue Number;** CID 515
**Produced By;** Daniel Lannois.
**Release Date;** 1992
**Highest Chart Position;** 7.
**Weeks On Chart;** 6.

**Title;** *Even Better Than The Real Thing.*
**Format;** 7"/12" and CD Single.
**Other Tracks;**
**7";** *'Salome'*
**12";** *'The Lady With The Spinning Head'/'Where Did It All Go Wrong'*
**CD Single;** (As above)
**Produced By;** Daniel Lannois.
**Release Date;** 1992.
**Highest Chart Position;** 12.
**Weeks On Chart;** 7.
**Additional Information;** A hugely popular and widely available, (charting in its own right) CD Single of *"Even Better Than The Real Thing'* was made available, and was particularly popular in the clubs. This comprised of five remix versions of the song under the following titles:-
1. The Perfecto Mix.
2. Sexy Dub Mix.
3. Apollo 440 Steal Sonic Remix.
4. V16 Exit Wound Remix.
5. A440 VS U2 Instrumental Remix.
(Tracks 1 & 2 were remixed by Paul Oakenfold, and tracks 3,4 & 5 by Apollo 440).
**Catalogue Number;** C REAL 2. 864 197-2.
This set of Remixes entered the charts in its own right reaching Number eight, enjoying a seven weeks chart duration.


**Title;** *Who's Gonna Ride Your Wild Horses.*
**Format ;** 7"/12" and CD Single
**Other Tracks;** Various remixed versions.
**Catalogue Number;**
**Produced By;** Daniel Lannois;
**Release Date;** 1993
**Highest Chart Position;** 14
**Weeks On Chart;** 6.

## ALBUMS

**Title;** *Boy*
**Track Listing;** *I Will Follow/Twilight/Into The Heart/Out Of Control/ Stories For Boys/The Ocean/A Day Without Me/Another Time Another Place/The Electric Co./Shadows And Tall Trees.*
**Format;** CD/LP/MC.
**Catalogue Number;** ILPS 9646.
**Produced By;** Steve Lillywhite.
**Release Date;** October, 1980.
**First Chart Entry;** *August, 1981.
**Highest Chart Position;** 52
**Weeks On Chart;** 31
**Additional Information;** *The album did not chart when first released, but subsequently did on the back of future successes.

**Title;** *October*
**Track Listing;** *Gloria/I Fall Down/I Threw  A Brick Through A Window/ Rejoice/Fire/Tomorrow/October/With A Shout/Stranger In A Strange Land/Scarlet/Is That All.*
**Format;** CD/LP/MC
**Catalogue Number;** ILPS 9680
**Produced By;** Steve Lillywhite.
**Release Date;** October, 1981.
**Highest Chart Position;** Number 11
**Weeks On Chart;** 41
**Additional Information;** U2's first entry into the British Albums chart.

**Title;** *War*
**Track Listing;** *Sunday Bloody Sunday/Seconds/New Years Day/ Like A Song.../Drowning Man/The Refugee/Two Hearts Beat As One/ Red LIght/Surrender/40.*

Format; CD/LP/MC.
Catalogue Number; ILPS 9733
Produced By; Steve Lillywhite.
Release Date; March, 1983.
Highest Chart Position; Number 1.
Weeks at Number 1; 1.
Weeks On Chart; 143
Award Status; Platinum
Additional Information; The group's first British Number One album

Title; *Under A Blood Red Sky*
Track Listing; *Gloria/11 O'Clock, Tick, Tock/I Will Follow/Party Girl/ Sunday Bloody Sunday/The Electric Co./New Years Day/40.*
Format; CD/LP/MC.
Catalogue Number; IMA 3.
Produced By; Jimmy Lovine.
Additionally Mixed By; Shelly Yakus.
Release Date; November, 1983.
Highest Chart Position; Number 2
Weeks On Chart; 201
Award Status; Platinum

Title; *The Unforgettable Fire*
Track Listing; *A Sort Of Homecoming/Pride (In The Name Of Love...)/ Wire/The Unforgettable Fire/Promenade/4th Of July/Bad/Indian Summer Sky/Elvis Presley And America/MLK.*
Format; CD/LP/MC
Catalogue Number; U25
Produced By; Brian Eno/Daniel Lannois.
Release Date; October, 1984.
Highest Chart Position; Number 1.
Weeks At Number 1; 2.
Weeks On Chart; 127
Award Status; Platinum.

**Title;** *The Joshua Tree*
**Track Listing;** *Where The Streets Have No Name/I Still Haven't Found What I'm Looking For/With Or Without You/Bullet The Blue Sky/ Running To Stand Still/Red Hill Mining Town/In God's Country/Trip Through Your Wires/One Tree Hill/Exit/Mothers Of The Disappeared.*
**Format;** CD/MC/LP
**Catalogue Number;** U26
**Produced By;** Daniel Lannois/Brian Eno
**Release Date;** March, 1987.
**Highest Chart Position;** Number 1.
**Weeks At Number 1;** 2.
**Weeks On Chart;** 113
**Award Status;** Platinum.


**Title;** *Rattle And Hum*
**Track Listing;** *Helter Skelter/Van Dieman's Land/Desire/Hawkmoon 269/ All Along The Watchtower/I Still Haven't Found What I'm Looking For/Freedom For My People/Silver And Gold/Pride (In The Name Of Love...)/Angel Of Harlem/Love Rescue Me/When Love Comes To Town/Heartland/God Part II/The Star Spangled Banner/Bullet The Blue Sky/All I Want Is You.*
**Format;** CD/LP/MC.
**Catalogue Number;** U27
**Produced By;** Jimmy Lovine
**Release Date;** October, 1988.
**Highest Chart Position;** Number 1.
**Weeks At Number 1;** 1.
**Weeks On Chart;** 47
**Award Status;** Platinum.


**Title;** *Achtung Baby*
**Track Listing;** *Zoo Station/Even Better Than The Real Thing/One/ Until The End Of The World/Who's Gonna Ride Your Wild Horses/So Cruel/The Fly/Mysterious Ways/Tryin' To Throw Your Arms Around The World/Ultra Violet (Light My Way)/Acrobat/Love Is Blindness.*
**Format;** CD/LP/MC
**Catalogue Number;** U28
**Produced By;** Daniel Lannois.
**Additional Production;** Brian Eno,

**Release Date;** November, 1991.
**Highest Chart Position;** Number 1.
**Weeks On Chart;** 63*
**Award Status;** Platinum.
**Additional Information;** *Album still in chart at time of going to press.

# COMMERCIALLY RELEASED PROMOTIONAL
# VIDEOS FOR ACCOMPANYING SINGLES

**Title;** *'I Will Follow'*
**Year;** 1981.
**Location;** Filmed live onstage in America.
**Title;** *'Gloria'*.
**Year;** 1981.
**Directed By;** Meiert Avis.
**Location;** Filmed on a barge in Dublin.


**Title;** *'A Celebration'*
**Year;** 1982.
**Directed By;** Meiert Avris,
**Location;** Filmed around The Kilmainham jail in Dublin.


**Title;** *'New Years Day'*
**Year;** 1982.
**Directed By;** Meiert Avis.
**Location;** Filmed on a snow-clad Swedish mountainside.


**Title;** *'Two Hearts Beat As One'*
**Year;** 1983.
**Directed By;** Meiert Avis.
**Location;** Filmed around Montmartre in Paris.


**Title;** *Pride (In The Name Of Love)* *
**Year;** 1984.
**Directed By;** Donald Cammell.
**Location;** Filmed in St. Francis Xavier Hall, Dublin.
**\*Additional Information;** Two other videos were also filmed for
the *'Pride'* single, but this version was, and still is the most com-
monly used and seen.

**Title;** *'The Unforgettable Fire'*
**Year;** 1985.
**Directed By;** Meiert Avis.
**Location;** Sweden and various other locations.


**Title;** *'With Or Without You'*
**Year;** 1987.
**Directed By;** Meiert Avis and Matt Mahurin.
**Location;** Dublin.


**Title;** *'I Still Haven't Found What I'm looking For'*
**Year;** 1987.
**Directed By;** Barry Devlin.
**Location;** Filmed around various spots in Las Vegas.


**Title;** *'Where The Streets Have No Name'*
**Year;** 1987.
**Directed By;** Meiert Avis.
**Location;** Filmed on a rooftop, (and the ensuing chaos it caused), in Los Angeles.


**Title;** *'Desire'*
**Year;** 1988.
**Directed By;** Richard Lowenstein.
**Location;** Filmed in various locations in America.


**Title;** *'Angel Of Harlem'*
**Year;** 1988.
**Directed By;** Richard Lowenstein.
**Location;** Filmed in New York.

**Title;** *'When Love Comes To Town'*
**Year;** 1989.
**Directed By;** Phil Joanou.
**Location;** Various.
**Additional;** Duet with B.B. King.
**Title;** *'All I Want Is You'*
**Year;** 1989.
**Directed By;** Meiert Avis.
**Location;** Filmed on the outskirts of Rome.

**Title;** *'The Fly'*
**Year;** 1991.
**Directed By;** Ritchie Smith and Jon Klein.
**Location;** Filmed in both London and Dublin.

**Title;** *'Mysterious Ways'*
**Year;** 1991.
**Directed By;** Stephane Sednaoui.
**Location;** Filmed in Morocco.

**Title;** *'One'*
**Year;** 1991
**Directed By;** Data not available at time of going to press.
**Location;** Data not available at time of going to press.

**Title;** *'Even Better Than The Real Thing'*
**Year;** 1992
**Directed By;** Data not available at time of going to press.
**Location;** Data not available at time of going to press.

**Title;** *'Who's Gonna Ride Your Wild Horses'*
**Year;** 1993
**Directed by;** Data not available at time of going to press.
**Location;** Data not available at time of going to press.

# OTHER COMMERCIALLY PRODUCED
# PROMOTIONAL VIDEOS
# (NON UK SINGLE RELEASE)

**Title;** *'Sunday Bloody Sunday'*
**Year;** 1983.
**Directed By;** Gavin Taylor.
**Location;** Filmed at the groups concert at The Red Rocks stadium, Denver, Colorado.

**Title;** *'Pride' (In The Name Of Love). (Version 2).*
**Year;** 1984.
**Directed By;** Barry Devlin.
**Location;** Filmed at Slane Castle near Dublin.

**Title;** *'Pride' (In The Name Of Love). (Version 3).*
**Year;** 1984.
**Directed By;** Anton Corbijn.
**Location;** Filmed in London.

**Title;** *'A Sort Of Homecoming'*
**Year;** 1984.
**Directed By;** Barry Devlin.
**Location;** Filmed in and around the following locations, Glasgow, London, Paris, Rotterdam and Brussels.

**Title;** *'Bad'*
**Year;** 1984.
**Directed By;** Barry Devlin.
**Location;** A live version of the song with its accompanying footage being taken from various locations.

**Title;** *'Red Hill Mining Town'*
**Year;** 1987.
**Directed By;** Neil Jordan.
**Location;** Filmed in London. The anticipated single release of this track from the *'Joshua Tree'* album never occurred.

**Title;** *'Night And Day'*
**Year;** 1990.
**Directed By;** Wim Wenders.
**Location;** Filmed in Berlin.

# COMMERCIALLY RELEASED LONG FORM VIDEOS

**Title;** *'Under A Blood Red Sky'*
**Year;** 1983.
**Directed By;** Gavin Taylor.
**Location;** Live performance from The Red Rocks natural amphi-theatre, Denver, Colorado.
**Track Listing;**


**Title;** *The Unforgettable Fire Collection*
**Year;** 1985.
**Directed By;** (Various).
**Locations;** (Various).
**Track Listing;** *'Pride (In The Name Of Love) (Version 1)/'A Sort Of Homecoming'/'Bad' (Live Version)/'The Unforgettable Fire'/'Pride' (In The Name Of Love') (Version 2)/*- Plus a semi documentary style film; 'The Making of *The Unforgettable Fire.*


**Title;** *'Rattle And Hum'*
**Year;** 1987/1988.
**Catalogue Number;** VHR 2308.
**Directed By;** Phil Joanou.
**Locations;** (various).
**Track Listing;** *'Helter Skelter'/'Van Diemans Land'/'Desire'/'Exit'/ 'Gloria'/'I Still Haven't Found What I'm Looking For'/'Silver And Gold'/ 'Angel Of Harlem'/'All Along The Watchtower'/'In God's Country'/'When Love Comes To Town'/'Heartland'/'Bad'/'Where The Streets Have No Name'/ 'MLK'/'With Or Without You'/'Bullet The Blue Sky'/'Running To Stand Still'/'Sunday Bloody Sunday'/'Pride (In The Name Of Love'/'All I Want Is You.'*(Contains nine extra tracks not on the album version).

**Title;** *Wide Awake in America*
**Track Listing;** *Bad (Live Version)/A Sort Of Homecoming (Live Version)/ The Three Sunrises/Love Comes Tumbling.*
**Format;** CD Only.
**Catalogue Number;** Island 902791A
**Release Date;** July, 1985.
**Highest Chart Position;** 11
**Weeks On Chart;** 16
**Additional Information;** This was an American only release that first charted in the British Albums chart on the strength of its import sales. The demand for the album led to it being granted an official British release, on CD only, in 1987.

# SOUNDTRACK ALBUMS
## TO WHICH U2 HAVE CONTRIBUTED

**Film Title;** *They Call It An Accident.*
**Year;** 1982.
**Song Contributed;** *'October'*
**Additional Information;** A second version of the same song was added to the soundtrack album, with the addition of extra keyboard sounds, provided by Wally Badarou.


**Film Title;** *The Last American Virgin.*
**Year;** 1982.
**Song Contributed;** *'I Will Follow'.*
**Additional Information;** *'The Last American Virgin'* was one of those seemingly endless American soft core sex flicks which enjoyed a remarkably short cinematic release and has probably clogged up video stores the world over since.


**Film Title;** *The Courier.*
**Year;** 1988.
**Song Contributed;** *'Walk To The Water'.*
**Additional Information;** This song also appears on the B-side of the *'With Or Without You'* single.


**Film Title;** *Until The End Of The World.*
**Year;** 1990.
**Song Contributed;** *'Until The End Of The World'*
**Additional Information;** The group contributed the song which was to become the title track of the Wim Wenders film. Wenders had previously worked with the group when he directed the promo video for their interpretation of the Cole Porter classic *"Night And Day'* for inclusion on the *'Red Hot And Blue'* album and video project.

---

**Film Title;** *Captive.*
**Year;** 1987.
**Additional Information;** The Edge, along with Sinead O'Connor and Michael Brook, worked together to write and produce all the soundtrack albums material.

# OTHER ALBUMS AND PROJECTS
## TO WHICH THE GROUP HAVE CONTRIBUTED
## EITHER COLLECTIVELY OR IN A SOLO CAPACITY

**Title;** *Snake Charmer*.
**Artist/Project;** Jah Wobble.
**Year;** 1983.
**Contribution;** The Edge performs on three of the albums tracks.


**Title;** *Do They Know It's Christmas/Feed The World*.
**Project;** Charity single to raise money for famine relief in Africa, originated by Bob Geldof and Midge Ure.
**Year;** 1984.
**Contribution;** Bono and Adam take part in the making of the single and appear in its accompanying video.


**Title;** *'In A Lifetime'*.
**Artist;** Clannad.
**Project;** The album *'Macalla'*.
**Year;** 1985.
**Contribution;** Bono duets on and appears in the accompanying promotional video for Clannad's *'In A Lifetime'* single.


**Title;** *'Sun City'*.
**Artist;** Artists United Against Apartheid .
**Year;** 1985.
**Contribution;** Bono sings vocals and appears in the songs accompanying promotional video.

**Title;** *Artists United Against Apartheid.*
**Artist;** Artists United Against Apartheid.
**Year;** 1985.
**Contribution;** Bono writes and records the solo effort of the song *'Silver And Gold'* for inclusion on the Artists Against Apartheid album.

**Title;** *'Maggie's Farm'.*
**Project;** Live For Ireland.
**Year;** 1987.
**Contribution;** U2 lend their live version of the Bob Dylan song *'Maggie's Farm'*, for inclusion on the Live For Ireland album, recordedduring the Self Aid concert in Dublin during May, 1986.

**Titles;** *'Sweet Fire Of Love'* and *'Testimony'*.
**Artist;** Robbie Robertson.
**Year;** 1987.
**Contribution;** U2 play on these two tracks which were included on former *The Band'* member Robertson's first solo album.

**Title;** *'It's Christmas, (Baby Please Come Home)'*.
**Project;** *A Very Special Christmas.*
**Year;** 1987.
**Contribution;** U2 contribute their version of *'It's Christmas.' (Baby Please Come Home)*, for inclusion on a various artists compilation album, the proceeds from which went to The Special Olympics charity fund.

**Title;** *'Jesus Christ'*
**Project;** *'A Vision Shared'*
**Year;** 1988.
**Contribution;** U2 contribute the track *'Jesus Christ'* to an album of Woody Guthrie and Leadbelly songs, in aid of the Smithsonian Institute in Washington.

**Title;** *'Night And Day'*
**Project;** *Red Hot & Blue.*
**Year;** 1990.
**Contribution;** U2 record their interpretation of the Cole Porter classic *Night And Day'* for inclusion on the *'Red Hot & Blue* benefit album, all proceeds of which go towards the funding into Aids Research.


**Title;** *'I Still Haven't Found What I'm Looking For'*
**Project;** *'Earthrise'*
**Year;** 1991.
**Contribution;** U2 lend a recording of their classic song *'I Still Haven't Found What I'm Looking For'*, for inclusion on the benefit album, *'Earthrise'*, the proceeds of which go towards learning the greater understanding of destroying the world's rainforests.

Listed below are a number of highly collectible U2 records, and the estimated prices that they would sell for; (Estimated values are taken from - 'Price Guide For Record Collectors' by Nick Hamlyn).

**Title;** *U2:3.*
**Format;** 12"
**Tracks;** *'Out Of Control'/'Stories For Boys'/' Boy-Girl'.*
**Record Label;** CBS Ireland.
**Catalogue Number;** CBS 127951.
**Year Of Origin;** 1979.
**Estimated Value;** £100.
**Explanation;** This was a limited numbered edition, released only in Ireland, of 1,000 twelve inch singles in a generic orange CBS sleeve. There are also Red, Orange and White vinyl copies, which sell for about half the price, (£40-£50), and Yellow vinyl copies which would fetch around £20.

**Title;** *'Out Of Control'*
**Format;** 7".
**Record Label;** CBS Ireland.
**Catalogue Number;** 7951.
**Year Of Origin;** 1979.
**Estimated Value;** £30.
**Explanation;** Limited edition release in yellow vinyl.

**Title;** *'Another Day'*
**Format;** 7".
**Record Label;** CBS Ireland.
**Catalogue Number;** 8306.
**Year Of Origin;** 1980.
**Estimated Value;** £20 - £60.
**Explanation;** The price estimate varies so much as there were a number of different coloured vinyl releases of *'Another Day'*, (Yellow, Red, Orange, White), as well as a Black vinyl demo version. Consequently the value changes as to which copy you own.

**Title;** '*11 O'Clock, Tick, Tock*'
**Format;** 7"
**Record Label;** CBS Ireland.
**Catalogue Number;** 8687.
**Year Of Origin;** 1980.
**Estimated Value;** £30.
**Explanation;** Limited edition release in Yellow vinyl.


**Title;** '*I Will Follow*'
**Format;** 7".
**Record Label;** Island.
**Catalogue Number;** WIP 6656.
**Year Of Origin;** 1980.
**Estimated Value;** £30.
**Explanation;** Limited edition release in white vinyl. There was also an limited edition release of '*I Will Follow*' released in yellow vinyl, this would fetch around £25.


**Title;** '*I Will Follow*'
**Format;** 7".
**Record Label;** Island.
**Catalogue Number;** WIP 6650.
**Year Of Origin;** 1980.
**Estimated Value;** £20.
**Explanation;** One-sided Radio only Promotional release.


**Title;** '*A Day Without Me*'
**Format;** 7"
**Record Label;** Island.
**Catalogue Number;** WIP 6630.
**Year Of Origin;** 1980.
**Estimated Value;** £12.


**Title;** '*Fire*'
**Format;** 7".(Double-pack single).
**Record Label;** Island.
**Catalogue Number;** UWIP 6679.
**Year Of Origin;** 1981.
**Estimated Value;** £15.

**Title;** *Two Sides Live*
**Format;** LP.
**Record Label;** Warner Bros.
**Year Of Origin;** 1981.
**Estimated Value;** £100.
**Explanation;** This was an American only promo release, given in limited quantities to US radio stations, of a live recording of the group made at a concert in Boston in 1981. A similar recording was also made and distributed under the title *'King Biscuit Flour Hour'* of another Boston concert, (also featuring the band Devo), in 1981, and this would sell for a similar amount.

**Title;** *4 U2 Play*
**Format;** 4 X 7" singles.
**Contents;** Record One - *U2:3*
　　　　　　Record Two - *'Another Day'*
　　　　　　Record Three - *'11 O'Clock, Tick Tock'*.
　　　　　　Record Four - *'I Will Follow'*.
**Record Label;** CBS Ireland.
**Catalogue Number;** PAC1.
**Year Of Origin;** 1982.
**Estimated Value;** £120.
**Explanation;** This was an extremely limited edition release of all the group's first four CBS Ireland single releases in a specially constructed plastic wallet, all on different coloured vinyls.

**Title;** *Blood Red Sky*
**Format;** LP.
**Record Label;** Island.
**Catalogue Number;** IMA3
**Year Of Origin;** 1983.
**Estimated Value;** £50.
**Explanation;** Limited edition release of *'Under A Blood Red Sky'* in red vinyl.

**Title;** *Two Hearts Beat As One*
**Format;** 7" (Double-pack single).
**Record Label;** Island.
**Catalogue Number;** ISD 109.
**Year Of Origin;** 1983.
**Estimated Value;** £10.

**Title;** *'New Years Day'*
**Format;** 7" (Double-pack single).
**Record Label;** Island.
**Catalogue Number;** UWIP 6848.
**Year Of Origin;** 1983.
**Estimated Value;** £15

**Title;** *'Under A Blood Red Sky'*
**Format;** LP.
**Record Label;** Island.
**Catalogue Number;** US 1PR.
**Year Of Origin;** 1983.
**Estimated Value;** £25.
**Explanation;** Promo version with band interviews.

**Title;** *'War'*
**Format;** LP.
**Record Label;** Island.
**Catalogue Number;** ILPS 9733.
**Year Of Origin;** 1983.
**Estimated Value;** £50.
**Explanation;** Limited edition release of *'War'* as a picture disc album.

**Title;** *Under A B*
**Title;** *Pride (In The Name Of Love).*
**Format;** 7'.
**Record Label;** Island.
**Catalogue Number;** ISP 202.
**Year Of Origin;** 1984.
**Estimated Value;** £20.
**Explanation;** Limited edition release of 'Pride' as a picture disc single.

**Title;** *U2. 2. Date*
**Format;** LP.
**Track Listing;** *I Will Follow/Two Hearts Beat As One/Sunday Bloody Sunday (Live Version)/The Unforgettable Fire/In God's Country/Bad*

*(Live Version)/I Still Haven't Found What I'm Looking For* (Live Version)
**Record Label;** Island;
**Catalogue Number;** U2 2D 1.
**Estimated Value;** £30.
**Explanation;** This was a promotional Greatest Hits album, made for Radio use only.

**Title;** *'The Unforgettable Fire'*
**Format;** 7".
**Record Label;** Island.
**Catalogue Number;** ISP 220
**Year Of Origin;** 1985.
**Estimated Value;** £20.
**Explanation;** Limited edition release of *'The Unforgettable Fire'* 7" single as a Shaped Picture Disc.

**Title;** *The Joshua Tree Singles*
**Format;** Boxed set of 5 X 7' singles.
**Record Label;** Island.
**Year Of Origin;** 1987.
**Estimated Value;** £100

**Title;** *'Night And Day'*
**Format;** 12" Promotional Copy.
**Record Label;** Island.
**Catalogue Number;** RHB1.
**Year Of Origin;** 1989.
**Estimated Value;** £70.

**Title;** *'Zoo Station'*
**Format;** 12" Promotional Copy - Picture Disc.
**Record Label;** Island.
**Year Of Origin;** 1992.
**Estimated Value;** £80.

# WITTICISMS

(U2 quoted through the years).

Bono on;

## (Religion )

*"Tis better to be drunk on the holy spirit, but sometimes Jack Daniels is handier".*

## (REM's Michael Stipe )

*'He's kind of like a Bing Crosby for the nineties isn't he."*

## ( On Achtung Baby)

*"If people didn't like the last album, they won't like what's coming"*

*"Most surprising moment of the tour?  When people bought the tickets"*

## (On what has kept them together)

*"Fear of our manager".*

## (On the infamous 'One' video)

*"Us in drag? Edge Looked like Winnie The Witch, Adam looked like the Duchess of York, Larry looked like an extra from some skin flick and I (Bono) looked like Barbara Bush."*

**(On the early days)**

*"We were so bad at playing other peoples' songs that we had to learn to write our own."*

**(On drugs)**

*"If I start talking about drugs I'm going to have customs officers up my bum every time I come into the country."*

**(On success)**

*"Success was like a big bad wolf. Now we laugh at it - the police escorts, the limos, etc. I used to find it embarrassing, now I find it funny, but you've got to enjoy the ride, its a trip."*

*"Well somebody's gotta play at being Rock 'N' Roll stars."*

**(Bono at the Brit awards when asked by an Israeli journalist if he had ever visited his country)**

*"Yes. About 4,000 years ago!"*.